FINDING YOUR VOICE

FINDING YOUR VOICE

A Practical and Spiritual Approach to Singing and Living

CAROLYN SLOAN

New York

ISBN: 0-7868-8388-X

FIRST EDITION

Designed by Chris Welch

Drawings by Yakov Leytush

10 9 8 7 6 5 4 3 2 1

To my students, who have taught me how
to teach with love and wisdom.

And . . .

To my husband Stuart and my son Samuel,
who give me cause to sing every day.

ACKNOWLEDGMENTS

I wish to thank the following people for their help and guidance in the production of this book:

My agent, Susan Golomb, for believing in me and the idea for *Finding Your Voice* from the beginning; Leigh Haber, my editor, for tirelessly tending to the book throughout its development and production; Beverly Willett for her sage legal counsel; Stacey Luftig for her introduction to Susan and help with the proposal; Rebecca Loveszy at New York University's music therapy department for helping me to connect with knowledgeable music therapists; Connie Tomaino of Beth Abraham Hospital, Dr. Amy Hammell of New York Hospital and Tina Brescia of the Rusk

Institute for sharing their ideas and feelings about music and self-transformation; Cantor Robert Abelsohn and Mark Kligman of Hebrew Union College and Father Steven Connor of St. Paul the Apostle Church for speaking to me about the religious and historical importance of vocal music; Joe Simmons, Diane Austin, Louise Montello, Susan Gregory, Barbara Hohenberg, and all the others who took time out of their busy days to talk to me and discuss the power of singing; Robin Berkowitz for her insightful preliminary editing; my husband Stuart for staying up late with me and listening to draft after draft.

I also wish to thank Andrea Maybaum and Shelly Wilson for their loving, tender care of my son Sam while I was away writing; everyone at Hyperion for publishing and distributing *Finding Your Voice* and helping to make it available to anyone who feels the need to sing.

I am greatly humbled and appreciative. Thank you.

CONTENTS

A Song — xi

Introduction — 1

1. The Power of the Voice — 7
2. A Visit with Three Students: M.G., Katie, and Gregg — 17
3. What You'll Need — 33
4. The Warrior — 39
5. The Scientist — 59
6. The Detective — 101
7. The Spiritual Master — 129
8. The Singer — 147

Epilogue — 171

A Song

I sang a song yesterday.
I thought I sang it well.
The notes were all in tune.
The phrases smooth and uninterrupted by unconscious breaths.
I varied the rhythms and spoke the words clearly.
I anticipated each key change.
My voice was warm and moved effortlessly through each rise and
fall of the melody.
When I finished, I was sure I'd told the story well and communicated
my interpretation.
But I did not experience a feeling.
My heart remained unchanged.
I was unmoved.
My soul still yearned for expression.
Despite my efforts,
I realized I had not sung at all.
The music, it seemed, slept quietly beside me,
patiently waiting to to be awakened.
I decided to start again.
This time I did not listen.
I did not watch.
I did not think.
This time I willingly vanished.
This time I became . . .
a song.
—*Carolyn Sloan*

FINDING YOUR VOICE

INTRODUCTION

Late one night, my son awakes crying and I enter his room softly. "What's wrong?" I ask. The crying persists and I start to sing to quiet him. "Twinke, twinkle little star . . ." He whimpers, "Mommy" and settles down. I continue to sing. He's asleep before long and so I return to my bed to do the same.

From the time I was a child singing has been a part of my life. I used to ride in the car with my father and sing every billboard I could see.

In high school and college I'd write and perform my own songs. Since then I've worked in nightclubs and recording studios singing everything from "Melancholy Baby" to Weight Watchers jingles.

Now I sing to my son, and share my knowledge and experience of song, of voice with others, as a voice teacher and coach. I am a singer. I allow myself to be sensitive to my environment, and therefore am moved by music and express what I feel by using my voice in song. But for me, the title "singer" has been hard won. For years I refused to refer to myself that way for fear I was not "good enough" to own it. Not good enough? What I really meant was I didn't feel my voice matched up to those voices I heard on the radio, or the voices I heard singing on Broadway. Everywhere I went, I carried with me a critical voice that told me I was not good enough and that silenced me. Needless to say, this inner critic made me miserable.

Confused as to what to do next, I went to my father, who was a singer himself, for advice. He suggested formal study, so for the next ten years I studied with opera singers, and teachers of classical technique. I studied bel canto, folk, and even tai chi in hopes of freeing my mind and body and building stamina. I studied creative visualization. I studied and studied. After all of this I asked myself if I sounded closer to being the kind of singer I wanted to be. I realized the answer was no. But maybe I was happier, more fulfilled? Unfortunately, I was not. Then exactly what had I accomplished? I couldn't answer that question. As it happened, it was at that moment that I stopped studying. I was offered a job working nights at a law firm, a world away from music. A galaxy away from my heart. But after all, hunger is powerful and I was poor. I needed a job. So I took it.

I edited contracts by night and wrote songs during the day. I was almost enjoying myself. And what started to happen as I wrote songs was that I was forgetting to listen to myself singing. I was simply singing to accomplish the task of writing a melody. For the first time I began to use my voice as an instrument. And because I wasn't really listening to myself sing, I also wasn't criticizing myself or self-consciously adjusting my sound. Of course, as this was happening, I was becoming a better singer, but that insight is all in retrospect.

Now that I had begun to think of myself as a songwriter, I acquainted myself with various musical styles: pop, R&B, rock, and folk. Each required me to sing a little differently and so out of necessity I experimented with my voice until I felt satisfied with a particular piece. Then one day as I was working out a section in a song, I found myself sort of scatting a melody line in a rather unusual range for me. Each time I sang the line, my voice responded by singing higher and higher. I went to the piano to double check my range, to see exactly what notes I was singing. Much to my surprise, I discovered I'd hit a high A, which I had never even approached singing before. How did I do it? I wondered. I realized I had no idea. I sang the phrase again and again until I began feeling the note as it sounded inside me. I noticed the note consistently landed in the same place ... at the crown of my head. I started singing other tones, decidedly lower ones, to see if I could do the same thing ... feel the notes inside me. Could I feel where I was singing them? Where did they vibrate? Ah ha! I thought, this is what voice placement is. Voice placement ... a term I had heard a lot about but had never been able to apply. I'd known how to define it: the location of the resonation of a particular pitch, but now I realized this location could actually be felt. You didn't need to hear it. Wow! How had I missed that one? Was I absent that day? In any case, now I understood and I was eager to test and retest my finding. My results were consistent: The higher the note, the higher the placement in the body. The lower the note, the lower in the body it would ring. Simple. Right? Not really. There was one large catch: In order for me to pull it off I needed willingness to be open and allow the experience to occur without controlling it; otherwise I'd miss. That's a hard one. I still hadn't figured out whether I could then monitor my voice objectively without trying to adjust it.

It was really then that my true course of voice study started. Ignited by an "accidental" discovery, I was on my way to truly teaching myself (and later, others) how to sing more proficiently, more effectively and truer to my own voice and character. I realized that *a voice is like a life. When it is freed and allowed to resonate in its natural channels, beauty abounds. If it is forced, manipulated or controlled in any willful, arbitrary manner, the voice—the life—withers and eventually loses its innate energy and dies.*

What I am describing here is the need for authenticity. A voice is as unique as the person it belongs to, and in order to truly sing, that fact needs to be respected, even as we are told that our voices should conform to some idealized form of singing. Years ago, I found myself caught in a common trap, thinking there is only one correct way to sing. In fact, there is one way . . . *your way!* . . . your voice, your work, your life. You must take responsibility for sailing the ship. There I was for years running to every other singer I could find for help, when ironically, becoming a better singer came down to trusting my own abilities, to finding my own voice.

The singers we love to listen to know this instinctively. They allow themselves to emerge through their voices. We love to listen to them in part because they teach us to be ourselves by supplying us with an example of genuine emotion expressed through song. By teaching us acceptance and speaking for us when we feel mute, they effectively unite us with ourselves. These great singers prove that powerful singing is about individuality, separateness, and even courage—it is not about a perfect voice. A singer needs to be a warrior.

I have learned that singing is about self-examination and observation, though not self-criticism. For example, where does the pitch sound when I sing it this way? How does it ring when I close my mouth a little sooner? A singer must be aware, be willing to experiment. A singer must be a scientist.

Along with courage and an ability to question, experiment, and observe, a singer also must have an unfailing persistence and desire to solve what may seem to be unsolvable mysteries. Why does my throat close every time I sing that note? What is it that makes my breath so unsteady when I reach the end of a particular phrase? Why am I afraid to sing ballads? A singer cannot afford the luxury of trusting only another's set of ears to decipher and remedy problems such as these. A singer must become his or her own ally, searching for clues and solving these mysteries for him or herself. A singer needs to become a detective.

Finally, singing teaches us we must temper our willfulness and transform it into purposefulness. "I'm going to hit that note. I will. I will." Each time we push, we fail. We fall short of the pitch or we sing it but somehow it lacks the beauty and grace we imagined it would have. We must balance our need to control with a necessity to let go so our true voices can surface. We do not create the voice. The voice is and creates us. It teaches us that we must be open to being stimulated and to experiencing our lives without inhibition. As a singer, it is imperative to be a spiritual master.

Does this sound like a tall order? I suppose it is. Learning to sing demands that we learn to be whole—for as we change, our voices reflect those changes and vice versa. I invite you to join me on this journey of becoming . . . of finding yourself . . . of finding your voice.

CHAPTER ONE

THE POWER OF THE VOICE

As the most common and instinctual form of music making, singing has had the widest possible links to other human activities, the singer having been at times also priest, healer, actor, poet, and much else.[1]

When we enter the world, we do so, not silently, but with a cry, a pronouncement of arrival—"I am here!" Before we can speak, we moan, we babble. We fill the air with our own voices, feeling ourselves vibrate, enjoying the sensations that our own bodies create. *We are our first song.* Every syllable, every coo, every heartbeat and pair of hands clapping, every set of lips humming, every breath, every cry creates yet another movement in the song of life. We are music. Music is our birthright.

[1] *The New Harvard Dictionary of Music* edited by Don Michael Randel, The Belknap Press of Harvard University Press, Cambridge, Mass., and London, England, 1986, p. 749.

Why then do we forget this power as we grow older? Why do we silence ourselves, and quiet our children? Why do we seem to lose touch with our own rhythm and our own voice? The amount of stimulation we receive from external sources is overwhelming. We are constantly bombarded with slogans, and advice from "experts" about how to relax, how to eat, how to sleep, how to raise our children and how to live. We are taught from early on not to listen to ourselves but to focus on other people, places, or things outside of ourselves as sources of comfort and wisdom. We learn to discount our inner voices, and in doing so we lose touch with ourselves.

Singing can and does reawaken what has been tucked away. It brings back into the light all our memories, dreams, tensions, conflicts, confidences, and insecurities. It connects us to a deeper place within ourselves because *sound is feeling.* Think about it. When you sing, or even speak, you vibrate. Air breathed in is let go and passed through your vocal folds, and like two plucked strings, they release a set of vibrations which in turn set off other sets of vibrations (see chapter 5, The Scientist). Vibrations are not only heard, they are felt. They are felt not only by the passive listener but by you, the singer. These sensations, like most "feelings," speak to us in a way that is not intellectual. These "feelings" can conjure mental pictures, reveal past events and sometimes teach us things about ourselves we were previously unwilling to accept. We cannot reason these feelings to appear. We cannot reason them away. They simply exist, even if they are waiting to be acknowledged.

I have a student, we'll call her Laney, who had been an alcoholic for much of her adult life. When she first came to me for lessons, she had been sober for two years. Through singing she began to discover all that had been buried for quite some time.

During one lesson she said, "I'm looking for a way out of my quiet mouse, good-girl voice. I'm sure I'm stuck on this sound because my mother thought it was impolite to sing too loud in church." When she first started to sing, I could hear what Laney was talking about. A woman in good health and seemingly strong, Laney sounded timid, and unsure of herself. Her voice was soft and unsteady. There was a lot of breath escaping in each phrase she sang. Soon after that particular meeting I asked Laney what her favorite type of music to sing was and she replied, "Rock and roll and blues." "Okay," I said and pulled out a standard rhythm and blues song. "Great!" she said. She started to sing, and I continued to hear mostly her own reticence. I encouraged her to try something different: to open her mouth wide on the higher notes while breathing deeply. "Relax," I said. "Remember—this is for you." Just then Laney opened up. The high notes all matched her wonderfully full lower register. Her middle range rang with clarity and authority. She was thrilled and amazed at the power of her voice. I could see, however, that even after this breakthrough, Laney still felt a bit more comfortable holding back and singing quietly; she immediately chose a gentler song for our next session.

Change happens slowly and as time went on I witnessed Laney learning to let go of her "need" to be "nice" in many areas of her life, not just singing. The fact that she was becoming capable of a fuller spectrum of emotion supported a wider and more varied range of sound too.

I want to make it clear that that after fifteen years as a voice teacher and coach I do not set out to examine and/or change a student's particular emotional makeup or voice. I have found that these "changes" naturally happen as a by-product of learning to sing.

Every voice lesson I teach reminds me of this truth. When students who have had trouble claiming their own voices and making their own sounds finally discover that "Yes, I can do this, I can sing," their whole person changes. I have watched quiet children begin to gradually articulate feelings and thoughts as they learn to sing. I have taught aggressive children and watched them calm down and become more accepting of themselves and others. I have taught children whose poor senses of themselves interfered with their own ability to stand up straight and speak. In all of these cases, singing gave these children a means to express themselves. It gave them a voice, a way to be heard. *The body, the emotions, and thoughts are all one. Singing is holistic in nature. It supports our wholeness as human beings.*

It is no wonder to me now why most of my students have undergone some kind of personal transformation during our course of study. The work we do together engages our internal energy systems and utilizes all the senses. Each sound that's sung awakens a feeling. Each feeling triggers a memory or a thought. Each thought triggers an action. While we are singing, we open up fully to experiences that we were previously unaware of and feelings that have been habitually hidden. If you speak to any psychotherapist, he or she will tell you that "opening up" is more than half the battle in helping patients to heal and in effecting personal change in their lives.

I had a student, we'll call her Darcy, who, when singing a perfectly innocuous folk song broke down in tears.

"What's wrong?" I asked.

"It's my jaw," she said.

"Does it hurt?"

"*No.* But it's very stiff. I had surgery on it a couple of years ago."

I remained silent.

"I was attacked in my home," she said, still crying. "I was hit and my jaw had to be wired shut for six months."

Darcy had been studying with me for at least a year, but in all that time I had not heard this story. Somehow, because she was experiencing difficulty singing, she was able to acknowledge some of the sadness and anger she'd felt at the time of the attack and injury. Darcy continues to work all this through, and while she does, she loves to sing, healing herself in the process.

Singing aids us in grieving and soothes us when we're wounded much in the same way it helps us to celebrate. It encourages, if not forces us to release energy in a positive manner. A couple of years ago I unfortunately lost a much wanted and hoped for pregnancy and was devastated by the loss. It wasn't until I started *voicing* my feelings about it that I began to regain some confidence and feel happier. Voicing my feelings about it included talking to friends and family, and a professional counselor, along with singing my feelings every day. No one told me to do this. It was something I felt I had to do in order to heal my pain.

A student of mine recently lost her father and was equally distraught. But she told me that every time she sang, she began to feel more at peace with her father's death.

If you are familiar with songs belonging to the genre called the blues, you understand how valuable the song can be to one in pain. Think of the songs originated by the African-American slaves of several hundred years ago.

Slaves were not allowed to have musical instruments, so songs and dances were performed a cappella. They took their impetus from the many things Slaves dared not say to the master, and from the things they dared not do. —The Quimbys, Georgia Sea Island Singers, St. Simons Island, Gullah African-American Music.

Usually referred to as Negro spirituals, such songs as "Go Tell It On the Mountain" and "Amen" have become mainstays of the American folk repetoire. Why have they established themselves in our consciousness to such a degree? Obviously they have continued to be sung and preserved for historical reasons but perhaps more important, they help connect us to the experience of deep loss, of profound disappointment, of some rude awakening that perhaps shook our confidence, disturbed our peace of mind and in some way changed our lives. At times spoken words are not enough to deal with and express the enormity of the pain we are feeling, and it is then that words and music have the most meaning. This music gives voice to our despair.

There's this ability in music, to reach the innermost self and by making that connection, music provides a revelation for the individual—that's where the transformation comes. Whatever it is about the music and however it's processed, there's this capacity that music has to touch us at the core of who we are, and to help us retrieve things, be it speech, memories, or physical abilities. —Connie Tomaino, Music Therapist, Beth Abraham Hospital, New York.

Sometimes singing is not only a release of energy, but a transformation of energy as well. My young son Sam sings to comfort himself when he is upset or hurt in some way. He'll take a tune that he's heard before and sing na, na, na, la, la, la, repeatedly until some change of mood occurs. Other times he'll actually sing himself to sleep. Singing has this effect on me too: the same effect experienced by a runner whose endorphins kick in just as he's ready to collapse; a singer too can experience a high. Singing has often made me feel stronger, happier, more alive, more positive in my approach to life.

For many cultures, singing serves just that purpose. The Hasidic Jews are an excellent example of a people who consider singing and music in general as inseparable parts of living a healthy, productive, and meaningful life. They use song recreationally and in daily prayer. They believe song is our most intimate expression. "To sing means to sense and to affirm that the spirit is real and that its glory is present."[2] When we sing, we are more likely to hear ourselves. And we are more likely to be heard. Hasidic rabbis have long said that the gates of song are right next to the gates of heaven and that "The one who sings, prays twice."

In ancient days it was customary to study and recite poetry, prayer and laws with aid of melody. For through the medium of melody, the meaning of the word became clearer and the text itself was more easily remembered.[3]

[2]"The Vocation of the Cantor" by Abraham Heschel, from *The Insecurity of Freedom* published by Farrar, Straus & Giroux, 1966, p. 245.

[3]*Biblical Chant* by A. W. Binder, Philosophical Library, New York, 1959, p. 11.

In Buddhism, chanting is an integral part of everyday life, including prayer. For every desire, there is a chant.

In the rural villages of South Asia, music is also an essential element in many of the activites of daily life and it again plays a prominent part in many cherished rituals. Within a single area, different social groups have their own individual songs which are passed on from one generation to another.

In the cities of Europe and North America, singing historically has been heard in a house of worship. Churches or synagogues were almost always filled with the sound of prayer in song. Places of worship were also traditionally the place where people would gather and commune with one another. Singing was and has been instrumental in helping to bring people together. And for anyone familiar with the Baptist sect of Christianity, you know how incredibly charged the service is because of the rocking gospel music.

Without going into a lengthy discussion about the history of Western music, I will at least say that the origin of music, vocal or otherwise, is based on religious forms. Johann Sebastian Bach wrote all of his chorales to be sung in church, of course. Handel's *Messiah* is a celebration of the divine. The origin of Western classical music is religious in nature. It was believed that song enabled worshipers to get closer to the Lord. Singing was considered a "sacred" art.

I'd like to change this terminology a bit, to make it a little less intimidating. I see singing as a "spiritual" art in terms of its emotional powers: The bonds and connections it can help build.

For example: Haven't you ever sung to your child? Haven't you shared time with a friend and by the end of the evening joined in a chorus of your favorite song? Haven't you chanted a familiar refrain at a football or baseball game? Or maybe in college you stood and sang in a chorus or marched, burning flags or bras, singing the songs of the times. Whichever applies to you I hope you can begin to see how *singing is a necessary art.* Whether you are singing a song with your best friend, or singing with a congregation praying, or a group of thousands at Madison Square Garden singing along to Billy Joel or the Spice Girls, singing is comforting in the way it supplies us with a common language. Music expressed through the voice instantly creates something meaningful, if not fun, to share. It helps foster a sense of community.

Whatever the reason, be it physical, emotional, psychological or spiritual in nature, singing is powerful. It affects us deeply, humors us, distracts us, and reminds us of our connection to ourselves and the world. Singing is an all-encompassing sensation. Our voices are unique instruments empowering us to experience, and to express ourselves. Our voices become music, and in turn, we can hear the music that is always present: the wind howling through the canyon, the ocean wave crashing against the rocks, the dog barking, the teapot whistling, the trumpet sounding and . . . *ourselves singing.*

CHAPTER TWO

A VISIT WITH THREE STUDENTS:
M.G., KATIE, AND GREGG

During the last fifteen years, I've witnessed some incredible personal transformations (including my own) as a result of teaching and studying singing. Students who were shy and withdrawn at first became more emotionally available. A woman who had had trouble voicing her wants and needs became more able to "speak up" for herself. Even children who were afraid to stand before a group of people became less frightened to do so and began voluntarily to perform.

The following accounts are a means of teaching by example. Following these "lessons" is an opportunity for you to think about and ask yourself some important questions. I encourage you to remain open. For when the student is ready, the teacher appears.

M.G.

RECIPE SINGING

Searching for a more facile voice, M.G. came to me, seemingly eager to discover new ways to improve her singing. She was a tall, athletic woman who worked on average fifty to sixty hours a week at a large business firm in New York City. She yearned to be a singer. She studied weekly, and practiced almost religiously. Given all of this, I anticipated that lessons would be productive and progress would be steady. I was mistaken and I soon came to realize that I faced a more challenging situation.

M.G. would come to her lesson and immediately turn on her tape recorder. We'd stretch and do our preliminary breathing exercises. We'd then proceed to the piano and vocalize. She'd sing an exercise, try to do everything "right"; she'd drop her jaw, sing using her diaphragm, and pronounce each syllable using accurate diction and phrasing. But there was an automatic quality to her singing, an unwillingness to participate in the moment. M.G. was so determined to get everything "right" that she wasn't feeling the sound in her body, and because she wasn't feeling the sound, she was really just listening to herself sing. By merely listening, she was letting her inner critic run the show, and I could see her adjusting her singing to fit her self-concept, instead of letting the singing come first. For her, this self-concept had her already being the professional singer she desired to be, therefore she wasn't really studying, she was performing. She was outwardly going through the motions but inwardly refusing to let go of old habits.

I tried to come up with a strategy that would reach her in a non-threatening way.

The next week I changed my approach. We started with a relaxation exercise and then slowly worked toward singing tones. I steered her away from traditional vocalizing, in favor of feeling sound; actually feeling the vibrations her voice would make by tapping on her chest, face, back, etc. Together we hummed low tones while tapping our chests, sighed long descending scales and worked on creating mere sound minus the perfectly enunciated words. Something powerful happened. M.G. started to cry.

"I can't feel the sound," she said. "I'm so frustrated."

I gently suggested she close her eyes and examine her body for any tension.

"I can't do this. I can't," she said. "I'm supposed to be good at doing this already."

"Doing what?" I asked.

"Singing," she said. "These sounds sound ugly to me. What are we doing this for?"

Judging by her anger, I knew I had struck a nerve. For the next fifteen minutes I couldn't get M.G. to keep working. Finally I was successful in having her relax and learn to feel the vibrations her voice made in her lower chest, though at the end of the session there was both a sense of relief and fear: relief that this "experiment" was over and fear of what we might face during our next meeting.

I'd asked M.G. to keep a journal during the next week describing her experiences while practicing. She was to make special note of her feelings and observations while also paying attention to her physical state. Was she feeling tense? Where was the tension? Did she want to cry?

The purpose of the journal was to keep her focused on asking and answering her own questions and solving problems, while taking the focus away from drilling exercises and listening too critically to her voice. With these things firmly established, I hoped that subtle changes would emerge, maybe not immediately, but within a month or so.

At our next meeting, M.G. arrived, seeming pleased and content. I asked to see her journal and she said, "Oh, I didn't see the point of writing it down. I can tell you about my week. Each experience was colored with ... 'It sounded good, I sang well, It was easy to sing the exercise because ...'"

It became plain to me that M.G.'s emotional investment was in doing things well and accomplishing tasks. As long as she felt okay about how she sounded, there was no need to delve beneath the surface. Of course this served her only as long as she was happy with her sound. If, however, she desired a certain sound and was unable to produce it, she immediately became impatient, frustrated, and unhappy.

I went back to the drawing board. How do I reach her? I asked myself. We again started with the relaxation exercises and low humming. M.G. closed her eyes and put her hand on her chest, and this time seemed more relaxed and ready to simply "play." I asked her to let the sound extend upward into her throat and mouth. She did so without much effort. By now M.G. was sounding more open, and things were progressing nicely. As she allowed the sound to resonate in her mouth, the sound changed. It became less guarded. I could almost hear a childlike quality ... an honesty that was new. I became very excited. Then M.G. started to cry. I didn't say a word. I waited for her to speak.

"I'm afraid," she said. "I'm afraid I don't know how to do this ... to let the sound go."

"I think you are doing it," I said.

"But I can't feel it. I mean, it feels trapped in my throat."

"What feels trapped?" I asked.

"My voice," she said. "It feels trapped—stuck."

"Stuck?" I asked.

M.G. folded her arms and looked down at the floor, holding her hands tightly clasped together. Then in a tiny voice she said, "I feel stuck. I'm stuck in a life I hate." She looked at me, stunned, as if she couldn't believe she was hearing the truth come from her own lips.

"Yes," I said. "Sing how that feels."

All at once, she let out a startling cry, singing, "I want to *sing. I want to sing.*"

"Sing it higher," I said.

Out came a gentle soprano, vulnerable and young. M.G. smiled. I asked her to sing it louder and louder. She released a low, breathy but confident, "I want to sing." I then asked her to sing, "I am singing. I am a singer." Once again she started to cry. Again, silence soon replaced the tears. By this time our hour was almost over. I waited for M.G. to make a sound, but she didn't. And then in a still smaller voice she cried, "I'm not a singer . . . yet."

"Are you singing now?" I asked.

"Yes," she said.

She looked up at me and smiled. Then as if she had heard an alarm bell ring, she turned her tape recorder off, closed her notebook and opened her knapsack looking for her wallet to pay me. I looked at my watch. An hour had passed. But I wondered why and how she had been so aware of the time when I myself was barely aware that it was time to stop. I resolved to start with a meditation next time. It was my hope to keep M.G. relaxed and ready to sing freely.

"Until next week," I said.

"Yes," she said. "Take care, I'll see you soon."

M.G. did not return the next week, nor did she call. I pondered the reasons for this, and the one I decided was probably most decisive was that I encouraged M.G. to be herself, in the process, inviting her to uncover aspects of her personality through her music. This process was obviously threatening and upsetting to M.G. to the point that not returning was the only way to cope with it.

M.G. was uncomfortable being a student and had difficulty accepting her own insecurity and frustration. But after all she was a competent adult, a professional, so why was singing so difficult? What could be the problem?

M.G.'s approach to study was what I call recipe singing. Tell me what to do, I'll practice every day and by doing what I'm told I'll succeed. M.G. was expecting me to change her without any deep emotional participation on her part.

Whether we are singers or not, all of us at times have been guilty of "recipe singing." Often, we wish others would take responsibility for us and show us the way. I warn you against this. You must blaze your own path.

Learning to sing or learning to sing better is never about learning by rote or strict memorization. If you find yourself craving answers and surefire methods for success, stop and ask yourself, "What is it that I really need now? Do I need someone to tell me how, why, and when, or am I frightened of trying to solve the problem myself? Am I uncertain of where to begin? Do I need more information?" If you can identify what it is that is making you feel insecure, you certainly will be on your way to solving the problem at hand. Make sure you do have enough information and instruction to support what you want to accomplish along the way but be sure to never let go of the fact that either you can be your own best ally or your worst foe.

As you continue reading this book, keep these principles in mind. I will bring them up again and again as a reminder to *trust yourself.*

Katie
IN SEARCH OF A BODY

It was late afternoon on a Saturday and I was waiting for my next student, a young woman named Katie. I imagined from her youthful phone manner and somewhat high pitched voice that she was a petite, soft-spoken woman.

At 5 P.M. the doorbell rang. As I opened the door, I was surprised to see a tall, heavyset, yet rather handsome woman standing in front of me.

I'm sure I looked stunned and was somewhat awkward as we made our introductions. In truth I couldn't believe how incongruous this woman's voice and stature were. "Let's talk a bit," I said. I invited her into the music room. "Tell me why you want to sing." I already knew why she wanted to sing from our phone conversation, but I really wanted to listen to her voice again, concentrating on hearing where she felt most comfortable resonating. As I listened, I heard her voice resonate in her mouth and face. There were no dips or inflections or brassy tones. There was no part of her speech that resonated anywhere near her chest or back. It seemed that Katie was extremely unaware of her body; each word sounded in the same place each time . . . somewhere above the sinus cavities. Everything beneath her head and neck seemed to be frozen and unknown.

"Let's go to the piano," I said. I was hoping to loosen her up musically. Maybe by hearing the music she would relax enough so her body could then be available to her.

"I'll sing a tone and you repeat it," I suggested.

As we started I could tell Katie was uncomfortable. The lower I went on the keyboard, the more tense she became.

"All right," I said. "Let's try singing some tones in the other direction."

The higher pitched notes were clearly easier for her. She sang them sweetly, with assurance, almost effortlessly. It was obvious to her and to me that she was much more comfortable in the higher register. I knew, in fact, she had once sung soprano in a choir.

But what I didn't know was the reason the lower pitched tones were so difficult for her, though it was apparent, that she had cut herself off from feeling vibrations below her neck, the part that would have produced the earthier, lower notes.

"Katie," I said. "Let's make sound. Let's not sing at all."

"What do you mean?" she asked.

"Let's just make some animal sounds to start. This is what I call my orangutan sound."

I proceeded to demonstrate. She laughed. I did it again. Once more she laughed heartily. Great, I thought. We're getting somewhere. As she began to join in, a new spectrum of sound was beginning to surface. Yet even in simply producing sounds, there appeared to be difficulty in reaching her lower register. As a matter of fact, I couldn't even detect a lower register.

"How do you make those low sounds?" she asked me.

"I don't know if you could say I *make* them, Katie. You might say I *allow them to emerge.* You have them too. Of course they're not going to sound identical to mine. You are your own instrument." Though she seemed puzzled by this, she also seemed receptive to trying again.

"Put your hand on your chest and talk to me," I said. She did. "How does it feel?" Do you feel a vibration, a kind of buzzing sensation?"

"No," she replied. "I'm not sure what I'm supposed to be feeling." I asked her to put the palm of her hand on my back. I sang a low pitch and held it for awhile.

"Wow," she said. "I can really feel your back buzz."

I smiled and assured her that soon she would be able to feel those sounds and vibrations in her own body.

The next part of the lesson was devoted to bringing her attention into her body. It seemed she had chosen to flee her body and regardless of the reason, it was imperative to get her back to living in it and feeling it again. We started with some basic yogalike stretching and relaxation exercises. "Tell me how your body feels as we do this," I said.

"It feels good," Katie answered. "I feel good."

"Take a deep breath, stretch your arms out, and tell me again." "I feel good," she said with her arms outstretched. "I feel really good." There was still little change in the timbre of her voice but I was beginning to sense much more freedom in Katie. She was relaxing and developing a sense of fun through the music as well.

In the ensuing months Katie became more and more willing to experiment and have a good time with her voice. I had suggested she find cartoon characters, animals, or other people she knew to imitate simply to help her open up. It worked. As long as she didn't have to focus on herself, Katie could let herself go. Her restraint disappeared and soon each lesson became an example of trust. She started making sounds that were drastically different. It was during a lesson where we were improvising melodies to a chord progression that she began to sing in quite a deep voice. "I'm gonna sing loud and take up the space I need. I'm gonna take what I need." The sounds were lower, more voluminous, and steady. Katie's speaking voice reflected the change as well. It was as though I was seeing and hearing Katie for the first time; even more important, Katie was *feeling and hearing herself* for the first time.

For some reason, Katie had felt an obligation to keep quiet all these years. It might have had something to do with her size; it seemed she'd compensated for her sense of being overweight by actually shrinking her voice. But as I had suspected, once she'd allowed herself to become "unconscious" of her physical state, she could begin to access more of her self, more of her voice.

It has long been my conviction that the voice is the channel to the soul. By working on the voice, the self will emerge and/or transform, and in Katie's case, the connection couldn't have been clearer. Her voice continued to get lower. Her self-confidence steadily improved, and interestingly enough, Katie also began to lose weight.

I enjoyed seeing how our voice lessons had become such an integral part of Katie's powerful transformation.

If you find or have found yourself in a situation similar to Katie's and are looking for a way to uncover a deeper sensory awareness of music, try asking yourself the following questions:

I. If I close my eyes, and clear my mind of any distractions, can I isolate the feeling in my feet? legs? torso? back? arms? neck? face? head?

2. If I can't feel these parts of my body with proper focus and concentration, could there be another reason I am not sensing these areas?
3. How do I feel about my body?
4. Do I enjoy physical activity?
5. What are my physical liabilities, if any?

(For example: I have trouble keeping my breath steady as I run. My stomach gets tense when I swim or stretch my upper torso.)

Your answers are keys to helping you grow as a singer. In later chapters we will do more of this, but for now, try to get acquainted with yourself and your feelings about your own physicality. Be sure to write down your answers and keep track of any changes you start to notice afterward.

Gregg
THE MISSING HEART

I was working at a music school in New Jersey when I first met Gregg. He was a young man who worked at a family business. He came to me with hopes of becoming a professional singer/ songwriter.

"I'm very successful at what I do," he said at our first meeting. "But I'd like to sing my own songs for a living." Gregg handed me a set of tapes he had recorded at home and asked me to listen to them.

I don't like to evaluate someone's original music but I was struck by the beautiful melodies and seemingly passionate lyrics.

Yet something was missing. I wasn't "getting" what Gregg was trying to communicate. And I wasn't exactly sure why.

I asked Gregg to sing a few of the songs he'd brought so I could hear again how he delivered them.

As he started, I could tell his voice was trained. It was resonant, true to pitch, and agile. His diction was close to perfect. So what was it that was missing? I couldn't tell whether Gregg was singing about working on the railroad or kissing his beloved. Gregg was not communicating. Again—what was missing? As I listened I knew. What was missing was Gregg and his emotions. But it wasn't until our next meeting that I had an idea of where to start working with Gregg.

When he arrived, I suggested we take a walk. While we walked I asked him questions about his life and family and work. I could tell work was easy to talk about. His tone was relaxed and he related his anecdotes with ease and laughter. When he spoke about his family, Gregg's jaw would tighten, his voice lowered and he never smiled. When Gregg spoke about his life in general there was ease but a kind of matter-of-fact quality that belied much of what I suspected Gregg was feeling. Not being a psychotherapist, I wondered what my responsibility actually was. I had no intention of delving too deeply, but since Gregg was having difficulty pouring his emotion into his voice and songs, I felt a certain obligation to help. I kept asking Gregg questions about his family. It was clear he was angry.

"Now let's sing," I said.

Gregg threw me a look of surprise and dismay.

"What about that song about leaving your lover? Let's do that one."

Gregg started to sing. And then quickly stopped. "I can't," he said. "My neck hurts. It's really stiff."

I suggested he take a couple of deep breaths and stretch it out.

"Let's start again," I asked.

"This is ridiculous!" he shouted. "I'm too tense."

"You sure are."

Gregg looked at me in a strange way.

"At least you know you're tense," I added.

"What are you talking about?" he asked.

"I can't understand what you're trying to say in your songs, Gregg. You're singing notes and words. I'm not sure what you're feeling."

"The words tell you what I'm feeling," he insisted.

"No they don't, Gregg. I'd love to hear the songs filtered through your heart."

Gregg stared at me.

"I don't know . . . I don't know," he said.

"Gregg, sing that song to me now. Sing it now."

This time when he started, the tone was rough, the pitch was good but his usual fluid voice halted. Did it matter? No. Why? Gregg's voice was now filled with emotion. I was moved because Gregg was feeling what he was singing. We had just had our breakthrough.

The coming weeks were difficult. Almost as a response to "too much, too soon" Gregg retreated. It wasn't until a month or so later that we got back to that first breakthrough. This time Gregg was able to "take in" what he was feeling and utilize this knowledge productively without a negative or fearful reaction. Soon Gregg's singing reflected the change.

"I see," he said. "All my feelings, even the ones I thought I was using in the song, were not there. I think they were kind of locked away. I wasn't using them at all."

"Right," I acknowledged.

"Maybe I was just explaining them."

Gregg seemed gentler now and ironically a little less self-assured. But what was exciting was Gregg's newly found authenticity. There was something about his emerging genuineness that was also reassuring. "I don't worry about how it sounds now," he said. "I just concentrate on what I'm trying to express." Astonishingly, these adjustments led to some seismic changes in Gregg's life. He left the family business for a job in the entertainment industry, a move he'd previously been afraid to make. He meditates on a regular basis, takes yoga classes, and works daily at singing as well as his sense of spirituality, which he now sees as being integral to one another.

There are times when we are all strangers to ourselves. Keep in mind that singing requires you to "wake up" to your emotions so as to arouse not only your own heart but the hearts of your listeners.

Spend some time with yourself every day. Try being quiet for just fifteen minutes and reflect on what's been happening in your life. Ask yourself how you feel about things. Are you happy? Is there a conflict you'd like to resolve? What could make your life happier, more productive? Are there any unexpressed feelings you need to share with someone?

Be nice to yourself. Tend to yourself the way you would a cherished friend or relative. It's important to "check in" with yourself daily. Unexpressed feelings have a way of blocking our natural impulses and getting us stuck. Our singing will reflect this if we are not careful.

As singers and musicians, we are communicators. The most powerful tools we have are those as simple as our hearts and souls. What powers music, after all, is our own emotion, our desire to communicate and the urgency and excitement with which we do so. It is up to us to be able to access these parts of ourselves with accuracy and grace, and most of all with love.

In chapter 3, you'll discover more about what you'll need to uncover your own resources. Through working with music and your own natural assets, you will find that with time, attention, and energy you can and will transform your voice naturally—and undoubtedly grow personally as well.

CHAPTER THREE

WHAT YOU'LL NEED

I n preparation for our musical journey, I urge you to consider this: Most activities in life require skill and training, though it is not for lack of skill and training that most people fail at these endeavors or quit before they have a chance to succeed.

Singing is no exception to this.

Failure is only sometimes due to a lack of training, and as a matter of fact in music, some of the best musicians were not "properly" schooled. Some cannot even read music. What is it then that causes us to succeed or to fail or to give up?

Have you ever tried to do something that you really didn't want to do? How long did it take you? How did you feel while you were doing it? Did it get done? Have you ever wondered why you can read that science-fiction novel twice as fast as you can balance your checkbook or write that long-postponed office memo? *What causes us to fail* or simply give up *is a lack of desire.* A lack of desire then becomes a lack of energy and a lack of energy causes our persistence to waver until it finally disappears altogether. Before you do anything, ask yourself, do I *really* want this? It's imperative that you be completely certain. Do I really want to learn to play golf, to speak French, to sing? Of course there are things that we *have* to do, like working, paying taxes, and various other compulsory matters. That is not what we're discussing here. What we are talking about is what we can choose for ourselves, be it our work, a hobby, or something purely for our personal satisfaction and fulfillment.

Music is demanding. It requires, much like living, your whole self. When you are sure of your intentions and the quality of your desire, the journey will be pleasant and the learning will be easier. So, the first thing you need to do is to make sure you have the true desire to open yourself up to your own voice. Desire is at the root of every successful action, no matter how simple or how complex. *Desire is your engine. It is your motivating force.* It will empower you. It will guide you and it will ensure your success in any endeavor. As a singer, desire will spark your imagination, increase your energy supply, feed your breath, and thereby increase your sound.

Here's how:

You conceive of what you want in your imagination. Your imagination houses your desire. Your desire (the picture of what you want) releases "energy." Energy is used to help manifest your desire. Now think of this in terms of singing. You hear a musical

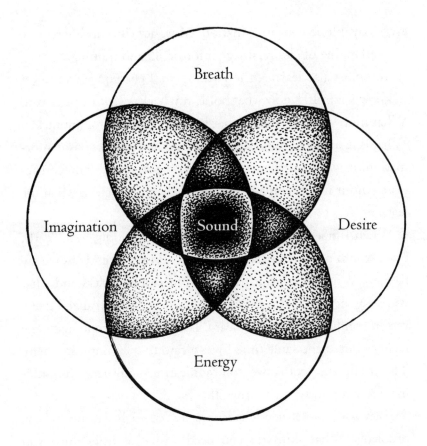

line (conceive of what you want). You wish to sing the music (imagination houses your desire), you take a breath (you store energy), you release the breath (release the energy). You sing. Imagination, desire, and energy become one with breath and sound.

Because desire is manufactured and born in the imagination, your mind becomes the control room for skill and training. Take a look at your ability to imagine. As singers, imagination aids us to place sound into the appropriate resonating chambers and to help ourselves relax. It also helps us to gently direct the muscles which govern our breathing. Make a point of dreaming a little every day. Hone your imagination. Most activities in life require an overlapping of desire, imagination, skill, and training.

You must also learn . . . how you learn. I encourage you to get to know yourself. Know what holds you back. What inspires you? What moves you to tears? What is it you want to communicate? What is it you need to release? Without knowing this basic information, it will be difficult for you to proceed with any conviction. And it will become even more difficult to persist when the learning gets tough.

When I first started to sing, I would sing loudly, and clearly, but I would never enunciate my words. People would always say to me, "You have a beautiful voice, but I can't understand what you're saying. What was that song about?" I finally realized that I was in conflict about being heard. I wanted to communicate my feelings but at the same time I was afraid to communicate them. The result was ineffective communication—unsuccessful singing. I was not in sync with myself.

Each song poses new challenges just as each day poses new problems. What skills do you need? What abilities must you have? As a singer, you need to know how to breathe efficiently, you need to expand your breath capacity, because without breath, there is no sound. You also need to suspend your disbelief. In order to accomplish what you set out to do, you must believe in yourself. You need an active imagination. The muscles which control your breathing respond only to visualization and sensory techniques. You need energy. Singing is very physical work. And without energy your breath will falter and so will your voice. You need to develop a good sense of pitch, if you don't already have one, because you need to be able to match a given frequency (carry a tune). You'll find that these things I've just mentioned are tools that remain constant. How you use them will vary; when you use them is up to you.

It is also imperative that you identify which of your personality traits are assets and which are liabilities. In my opinion, no personality trait should ever be considered a liability. Most of us don't realize this because we focus on the negative. "I'm too fat." "My nose is too long." "I don't have a college degree." "I have a terrible voice." These statements are excuses. They sap your energy and create stumbling blocks to growth and learning. Those who are happiest and most successful in this world accentuate the positive. If, however, you live your life being overly optimistic or terribly negative, you run the risk of seeing things and acting on them in an unrealistic fashion. Life is living in the middle—a balance between extremes. Try to avoid acting on these extremes. Knowing which situation requires what skill is important. In other words, think of yourself as many different people serving one person—*you*. Identify each day, each situation as an opportunity to meet the challenge using a different aspect of yourself. Develop your warrior, scientist, detective, and spiritual master and call upon them as you need them. I implore you to follow your intuition throughout. Trust yourself and enjoy the process. May you sing with all the love and emotion nature has given you.

THE WARRIOR

CHAPTER FOUR

THE WARRIOR

"Courage is making the first step."

A young boy, of about eleven years, stands alone atop a
small mountain. He is dressed and ready for battle, yet animal skins are all he wears and water and a knife are all he carries.
He has been directed to return home with the skin of the black
bear that lives in the cave in the mountain; a rather large feat for a
boy eleven years old. When night falls, he makes a fire and plans
his strategy. Alone, he must make the right choices to protect
himself and accomplish the task set before him. It is time to become a man in the eyes of his tribe and to prove to himself he is
worthy of the title, yet to be earned, Warrior.

During the night, the boy considers the many ways to capture
and conquer the black bear. But all ways seem dangerous. And all

ways point to the boy's likely death. Confused and frightened, he ponders his situation. Approaching despair, something strikes him, something an elder had said at a tribe meeting. "Wherein lies a difference, therein lies the answer." He realizes that to fight the bear would be foolhardy. After all, the bear is more than twice his size. He is a skilled fighter but the black bear certainly could and would overpower him. The way to conquer the bear is not to fight him—but to befriend him.

The boy devises a scheme. As he had done a hundred times before, he prepares some simple traps. He works quickly, capturing a rabbit, a fox, and a bird. He then howls like a coyote in the center of the woods, hoping to stir the bear. Sure enough, the bear comes lumbering forward. First the boy throws the rabbit, then the fox, then the bird. Finally, and all at once, the boy faces the bear.

Frightened, the boy stares into the eyes of the bear as he bends to the ground and picks up some berries that had fallen from a nearby tree. He then extends his hand full of berries to the bear. The bear bends his head forward to the boy's hand and eats. He seems pleased, and almost docile now. The young boy gathers more berries from the ground and begins to walk back to the village. The bear follows, occasionally eating from the boy's hand.

When the boy returns to his village, with the bear peacefully walking beside him, all are stunned, but proud. No one had expected such an unlikely outcome. It is true, the boy thinks later. "Wherein lies a difference, therein lies the answer." The difference was, the boy could reason and plan, as well as work on gut instinct, while the bear's only weapon was brute force. By exploring the difference, the boy was able to transform his fear into courage, therby completing the task and earning the title warrior.

Life challenges us every day with different problems and situations. There are instances that prey on our strengths and bring out our fears. Situations that require us to call upon our innermost resources in order to survive. Alone, we must face the difficulties that lie ahead at every turn, in every choice, every day. Each of us has a black bear we must confront. But how many of us choose to battle, and how many choose to flee? How many of us simply placate our adversaries, pretend our problems don't exist, or ignore the ones we know that do? It is the way we choose to battle or not to battle the "bear" that teaches us about ourselves and who we are.

I want you now to picture *yourself* a warrior. What images come to mind? Are you the young boy atop the mountain, dressed in animal skins, carrying only a knife and water? Do you see yourself a fighter-pilot in military uniform? Or a goddess of the earth bedecked in beads, feathers, and bells? Perhaps you don't see anything at all because you can't possibly imagine yourself a warrior. Well, it's time to start.

The warrior is not averse to doing battle for what he or she wants or believes. The warrior is willing and able to take the first step in any direction pointing toward a perceived victory.

Victory? Am I implying struggle, fighting, war? Yes. Even if the fight is not physical, and even if the struggle is quiet, the war is ongoing and the battle is raging. It is taking place with the armies we have nurtured in ourselves, in our fears and excuses, our artificial limitations, our self-created confusion and our own rigidity. "I can't do that. I can't hold a note for four bars. Never. It's impossible."

It's possible. Not only is it possible, it's probable that you can and you will.

Think of a song you love but one you feel you just can't sing. One in which there are too many high notes, or in which there are long phrases which demand an enormous amount of breath. Or one you wouldn't even dare to sing because, "I know I'll never sound like Whitney Houston!" (Or Frank Sinatra, or Sting, or Judy Garland—you get the idea.) Yes, I want you to choose a song laden with all of that fear, apprehension, and dread. This will be the song you work on throughout reading this book.

Yes, I know it sounds crazy. Why not pick something simple and straightforward? Because to foster growth, in singing as well as other areas of our lives, we need to welcome challenge.

As singers, we have lots of images of how we are "supposed" to sound. These images are mostly destructive. They're destructive because they've been based on who we think we should be and how we should sound instead of who we are and how we actually sound. It's necessary to be brave enough to let the images go. Be prepared to be surprised. You just might be a better singer than you think you are.

Noticing Reactions in the Body

Our first step in tackling the song you have chosen is to notice, in your body, how you react to this song or how you react to even the idea of singing the song. Does your throat tighten? Does your heart beat fast? Are your breaths short and nervous? Allow yourself to feel your body's reactions. If you can pinpoint a few, focus on these for the moment and remember them. (Writing them down is even better.)

Take into account, as we experiment and play throughout this book, that any inner criticism you inflict on yourself is very harmful. It will not only stop you mentally, but physically you will actually be stopping vibrations from happening. Criticism creates tension in the muscles. Tension in the muscles will restrict your breathing, which in turn will restrict the sounds you make. Restricted sound will then be judged as poor singing and the cycle will continue. Be patient with yourself.

A warrior's confidence comes in learning to master the tasks set before him. Before we can fully adopt the stance and bravura of the warrior, let's work on acquiring a few skills.

The Breath

As a singer, your breath is like fuel for your car—without it you can't move anywhere. It's the same with breath and sound. Little breath yields little sound. Unsteady breath, unsteady sound, and so on. Much as you might like to, you can't control the muscles that regulate your breathing in the same way you lift your arm to open a door, or in the way you put your hands together to clap, or in the way you open your mouth to eat. Sure, you can hold your breath and let it go, you can breathe in and out on command, but try speaking or singing when you are nervous and upset, or really angry, or sick with the flu. At these times your breath is not your own. It becomes the property of your physical and emotional state. How many of us have tried to blow out the candles on a birthday cake with only moderate success?

Technically, the organs and muscles involved in breathing are the lungs, diaphragm, and intercostal back muscles (see diagrams and more technical information in chapter 5, The Scientist). These muscles function in what is called a reflexive manner; a natural, automatic response to stimuli. In other words, your breath changes all the time—often without your awareness—as your emotions and physical condition change. For example, fear and anger make you breathe more shallowly, and a deep state of relaxation promotes deeper breathing. People who meditate, do yoga, and subscribe to the ways of a more "eastern" lifestyle have known this for a long time.

To take a look at how we and our voices work, we need to slow down. We need to *relax.* Why? Involuntary organs, such as the ones which control our breathing, are largely the servants of the emotions. And most of our emotions are usually closeted in our unconscious. Relaxation becomes key because when we relax, all the ghosts and garbage that have been lurking in our subconscious during the hours of the day and past days have a chance to visit with our conscious mind. It is here that we can deal with them, understand them, or simply get to know they're there. By knowing these "ghosts" exist, it becomes easier to place them in perspective, and we are then free to achieve a more peaceful concentration. Greater concentration yields a clearer mind, which then helps us gain control over ourselves and our voices.

In short, the first step in learning to sing better is to breathe more efficiently, and the first step in learning to breathe more efficiently is to learn to relax. Below are breathing exercises designed to help relax and empower you. While doing them, remember: As the warrior, let your instincts guide you. That's one of the warrior's primary advantages: an ability to work on gut instinct, on feeling. So let your body talk to you. Good singing is about knowing and feeling vibration in a physical way. As we all well know, we can't always hear ourselves correctly. Sensory awareness then becomes very important. So, get your head out of the way and let the sensations you feel in your body tell you what you need to do. In other words: Don't think. *Feel.*

As we progress in our journey of learning to improve our voices, it is important to remember that we are all different. If you are a medium-build person with a strong, prominent jaw and barrel chest, you will surely sound different from someone extremely tall and fine-boned with a receding jaw and narrow chest. (Chapter 5, The Scientist, will address scientific reasons in more detail.) Different instruments have different sounds. You wouldn't expect a tuba to sound like a violin or a trombone to sound like a clarinet.

Now, because we are all different instruments, the only proper way to monitor sound is from the inside out. "I couldn't reach that note, my throat got tight." Observations and statements like these will help you further down the road, when we get to figuring out why something went "wrong." Remember, a teacher listening to you can only give his or her experience as a model. You will learn best by examining and testing your own physical experiences.

Competition and Envy

About fourteen years ago, when I had very little of the self-awareness I have now, I went to hear a friend sing at a local cabaret. I was very moved by the beauty and clarity of my friend's voice. The next day, upon sitting down at the piano to practice, a cold sweat came over me. I wondered what this could possibly be about, but then tried to ignore my feelings. The first set of warm-ups went okay, but my throat felt tight and my palms were still damp. Again I ignored these "symptoms" and proceeded to practice. "Something's not right!" I felt. "It just isn't working. I don't sound right!" Sound right? What did I mean? I continued forcing the next couple of scales and exercises until I finally broke down in tears, remembering my friend's voice. At that moment, I realized my own envy and jealousy and strong desire to match those elusive sounds created by my peer. I was sure I would never sing again unless I could sound just like the friend I heard sing the night before.

While I clearly came to a crisis that day, I was probably in danger long before that. Why? Because I was searching for something outside myself—some sound that did not belong to me, that was not a part of me and was never to be created by me. And all the time I could have spent investigating my own instrument was instead used trying to imitate and recreate my perceived "perfect voice." I will add that many voice teachers may not usually notice when you are trying to match some pre-existing sound. They will usually try to encourage you to work harder. This only serves to make matters worse. Remember, your true voice can only be arrived at with a relaxed concentration and careful attention to individuality.

> NOTE: There is no perfect voice. There is no such thing as "recipe singing." Meaning, a given exercise may be good for one but not for another. You are your best teacher. We are each one-of-a-kind instruments. Learn to celebrate that. Trust it and let go.

Clarifying Your Purpose

Along the way, know that courage may lag, and determination may wane. At these times try to remember why you have chosen to sing. In other words, re-establish your sense of purpose. "I want to sing because when I am singing I feel beautiful." "I want to sing because I need to connect spiritually to the world and music helps me do that." "I want to sing because it helps me not smoke." Whatever the reason, remind yourself of why you want/need to sing. Why? Because *desire*, in addition to creating energy, creates a *purpose*. Purpose creates a path. And once the path is shown, we are unlikely to stray for too long. If we do, there will usually be a sense that something is wrong and/or that something is missing. Of course you'll have to allow yourself to sense that. And when you do, you'll realize "that something" is, of course, you and *your voice*.

BREATHING EXERCISE 1
Using Visualization

Lying flat on the floor, allow your muscles to relax, and close your eyes. Feel your body start to sink into the floor as you breathe slowly and comfortably.

When you feel all the tension in your body dissolve, bring your attention to your spine. Feel it lengthen and loosen against the floor. Make sure your mouth is slightly open and feel the breath slowly pass through your lips as you release it. Now imagine your breath flowing effortlessly from your spine up through your abdomen and chest, through your throat, and out through your mouth.

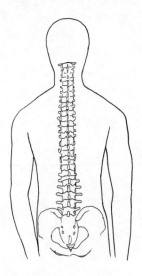

Bring your attention to your spine. Let it help you guide your breath.

Now picture a familiar place, one that you like and where you feel happy. Make sure to notice everything on the way to your destination. Notice the temperature, what you see, what you hear, how you feel and who you see, if you see anyone. Notice how your body is responding. Notice your breath. Has it slowed down or sped up since we started? When you answer these questions for yourself, make sure to register your feelings and make a mental note of them.

When you reach your destination, sit down and enjoy yourself. Again, take in what's around you and register how you feel.

Now that you're comfortable in this familiar place, imagine that place as if it were inside you. Take a deep breath, and bring what you have seen and heard and felt into your body. Actually breathe it in. Imagine it actually living inside you.

See that place housed deep down inside of you, residing somewhere beneath your ribs and above your lower abdomen. What does this feel like? Is it comfortable? How are you breathing?

In your own time you are going to let your breath deepen, touching that familiar place inside you. How does this feel? Let your breath tell you. Is it free and long? Does it feel tight and short? Enjoy the process and stay relaxed.

When you feel ready you will return to the room, allowing your breath to guide you back. Imagine yourself floating on top of this steady stream of air. You feel yourself embraced by it while it carries you effortlessly home. Be sure to notice what you feel as you return.

Open your eyes and stretch.

In a notebook or a journal, describe, in sensory terms, your experience. What did you feel, and where in your body did you experience these feelings? What did you notice about the breath? Were you aware of it and how much of the experience did you register? How was the trip back?

I encourage you to be specific about each experience. It is important that you learn to put into words exactly what and how you feel.

BREATHING EXERCISE 2

For Stretching Muscles and Creating Physical Awareness

Step 1. Standing straight, feet spread apart, arms at your sides, bring awareness to the spine and back. How does it feel standing in comparison to lying flat on the floor? Is there any tension or pressure in the body at this moment?

Step 2. Raise your arms and hands straight up, so that you feel a pull in each side. Continue by stretching arms up and over each side, one at a time, bending at the waist slightly from side to side. Be as flexible as you can without straining yourself.

Step 3. Drop your arms to your sides and relax for a moment. Inhale, exhale. Focus on a new area of your body, the head and neck. Picture a series of strings pulling your head up to the ceiling, beyond the ceiling and up toward the sky, up into the galaxy. Let yourself feel the pull in your neck and shoulders and at the top

Stretching head, neck, and torso.

of your spine. Again, it is important you be aware of any tension or pain. (Stop if you feel pain. It probably means that your muscles are tight and that you are straining yourself. Attempt to avoid injury at all times.) Try to keep your chin parallel to the floor during this exercise.

Step 4. Now roll your head gently from side to side, back to front, slowly. Never make a full circle from front to side, around back, to side to front, as this may strain the spine and compress the vertebrae.

Step 5. Raise each shoulder up and down separately, then rotate shoulders separately, with arms at your sides. How does this feel?

Step 6. To release tension in the spine, let your upper body roll slowly down until your hands reach your feet, keeping the back round, and bending your knees if necessary. Allow yourself to experience your own body and its own resistance during the course of this exercise. Pay attention to the particularities of your own body.

Step 7. Raise yourself up on your toes now, and then lower yourself onto your heels. Try it feet together, parallel, and then with feet spread wide apart, always bending your knees. In your notebook or journal, note your feelings and any difficulties you had with this exercise.

BREATHING EXERCISE 3
Breath and Vibration

Now let yourself make a sound. Don't make it music. Just make a sound. Make sure that the sound is low and voluminous, resounding somewhere near the chest cavity and/or behind the shoulders. You can check this by placing a hand on your chest. Let the sound grow in depth and volume. Any syllable is fine, but "uh" or "ah" might be best, as these tend to leave your throat most open. As you continue to make this low sound, notice what is happening. Do you feel freer? Do the vibrations in your chest come easily or with difficulty? Either is okay. Remember, you are getting to know yourself and your voice. There are no "supposed to's." Just notice the physical reactions. Don't judge them. Simply arrive at a sound, comfortably supported by breath and uttered from your body and soul.

Now let the vibrations travel. (Change the pitch and notice how the vibration moves.) Come back to the original sound (pitch), low, dark, and full. This is your warrior sound: true, full, deep, and uniquely you. This sound, vibrating close to your chest cavity, will serve as home base, a familiar place where sound is comfortable and arrived at with ease.

This sound, probably close to your speaking voice, is going to be stretched and challenged. It is the seed from which all other sounds will grow. It is important to tend

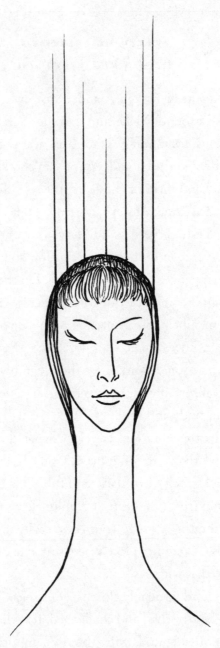

Picture a set of strings pulling your head up to the ceiling. Feel the stretch in your neck and shoulders and at the top of your spine.

to this seed. Focus on it. Feel it. Taste it. Let it ring. Recognize your body's responses to it as it sounds.

For many of us, this is the hardest thing to do. Often we discount the part of us that feels, in favor of the part of us that thinks. But great singing, or great living, for that matter, is about feeling and sensing, about intuition and instinct. Let the warrior govern you now. Otherwise, as I have mentioned before, self-judgment will create tension in the muscles. Tension in the muscles will restrict breath, which in turn will restrict sound. Restricted sound will then be judged as poor singing. Remember, in the beginning of learning to sing, or learning to sing better, the warrior is our first friend, and courage is making the first step.

Next, hum the first couple of lines of the song you have chosen to work on. Can you feel the motion of the line? Do you feel like you can create enough breath? If not, you can create mental pictures to help yourself develop your own breath capacity. I find the following exercise helpful. Remember to notice all of your reactions. Write them down. Be prepared to be surprised.

BREATHING EXERCISE 4

Supporting Vibration

Imagine a strong steady flow of air coming from the lower abdomen. Imagine this flow of air, like the wind, endless and powerful. Now picture something balancing on that air, "in the wind," that you don't want to fall. Direct that object, no matter what it may be, up through your stomach, chest, and throat right into your face.

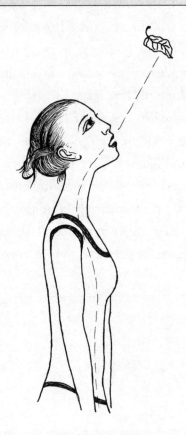

Imagine yourself balancing an object on your breath.

When you feel it present, hum. Leave your mouth slightly open and release that tone again. Feel the warm, slightly tickly feeling it creates in the front of your face. These are vibrations moving against the front part of your face. Keep this sound present and place your hands on the sides of your face by your cheekbones. Feel the vibrations while you hum. Do this until you become more acquainted with what the sound actually feels like in you. When you feel ready, let the wind inside you subside. Relax your face and body and stretch.

Did you feel the breath travel? How was it balancing the object? Did you let it fall? If it did fall, what did that feel like? Describe the sensations of the vibrations in your face. Did you feel any tension in your face, throat or body at all? If so, where?

Now open your mouth a little and sing on "la" a few lines from the song you chose to work on. How do you feel? Does the sound of your voice bother you? Does it sound good to you? Again make notes of how you feel. It's important to also notice whether you are hearing someone else singing the song while you are singing. Are you comparing your voice to another's? Are you criticizing yourself as you sing? Or is the discomfort merely mechanical? Be clear. Be aware. Without awareness we are trapped in our own doubts and fears about our inability to create the sounds we wish to make with our voices.

THE SCIENTIST

CHAPTER FIVE

THE SCIENTIST

"Your objective: physical proof."

t's 8:30 A.M. and I am feeding my son, Sam, breakfast. He picks up a lid from one of his baby food jars, extends his arm out over the side of the high chair and drops it. It spins as it hits the floor. He looks at it and smiles and then looks at me. Again, he picks up another, turns to the side and drops the lid. He looks for it after it has fallen. He is expecting the same results.

Later that day, Sam pulls a book from the bookcase, shakes it and listens for a sound. There is none. He tries again. Minutes later he picks up a toy bear that rattles. He shakes it and smiles at the sound. Then he looks back at the book, picks it up and shakes it again. Huh. No rattle. He seems disappointed. He tries again.

It is no surprise that children are curious. Everything is new. Every ordinary object is stunningly interesting. Each day supplies them with countless opportunities for obtaining knowledge and skills through play. They experiment, and through trial and error, learn firsthand what happens when you pick up Mom's shoe, lift it above your head and drop it. Children are natural scientists. They are always testing cause and effect. They are intrigued with the seemingly mundane and are fascinated enough to wonder. Questions "What?" and "Why?" are paramount.

As we grow older and more sophisticated, it is natural that we should lose some of our childlike curiosity and keen sensory awareness. But think about the last time you stopped to ask yourself how something worked or why it works the way it does. When was the last time you tried to do something familiar in an unfamiliar way just to see what would happen? If you're anything like myself, the answer to that question is "I don't remember because it's been so long."

In school we learn how to read. We learn how to add and subtract and we learn dates and time lines. We memorize the table of elements and if we're lucky we're taught to examine what happens when you pour a few drops of oil on the top of a glass of water (an exercise demonstrating the surface tension of water). But when are we taught to experiment in and with our own lives, do we take that elementary scientific training and apply it elsewhere? Are we encouraged to be inquisitive and creative and wonder what makes us who we are? Very rarely. Yet this is exactly what's necessary in order to *sing well* and in order to *live well*.

Singing as we have learned is a sensory art. It is also a precise science. The same is true of life. Both require us to be well-trained and experiment. Both require us to be present and aware.

As a voice teacher, I cannot experience things for my students. I can guide them, instruct them, inspire them, and love them—but I cannot feel what they themselves need to experience for themselves. For example, if I were to say, "Pay attention to the vibration in your chest. Feel it. Where is it?" they would put hand to chest, hum a little and try to experience that sensation the vibration created. Sure, I can also feel their vibration, but I cannot process it the same way they can. I can only share it second hand. I am a witness. Not a participant. Singing requires wholehearted participation. Much like living.

Taking Time to Wonder

It's time to reawaken your sense of curiosity and wonder. It's important to try to see things through the eyes of a child again. Ask questions. Make believe. Experiment. The most important thing you can do for yourself at this point is to forget you *know* anything. Approach your voice (and your life) as if it is brand new. Your scientist is defined by a thirst for knowledge. Without nurturing this attribute in yourself, your experiments will lack a certain diligence and enthusiasm. You must be passionate about the work—and be objective about the results. As Albert Einstein once said, "It is not the fruits of scientific research that elevate a man and enrich his nature, but the urge to understand."

SENSORY AWARENESS AND
OBSERVATION EXERCISE

In the morning when you awake, look around your room and notice everything in it. Look at your dresser. Look at a print on the wall. Look at the lamp beside your bed. Examine each of these things. Feel the texture of the lamp shade. Look under it at the lightbulb. Run your hand along the furniture. How does it feel? Could you describe it? What color is it? Does it change according to the light? What kind of sound does the light switch make when you turn it on? Observe your environment. Ask yourself the same questions about the same things in the same room but when the light outside is different. Perhaps get out of bed one hour earlier (or later). Does it change how the objects appear in the room? If it does, what is different about how the objects appear in the room? Next, listen to the sound of the morning. What do you hear first when you awake? Is it the sound of the alarm clock? Are there birds outside your window? Are they singing? How does the sound outside your window differ from the sound inside your room? Describe it the best you can. Keep a notebook handy and write these things down as they occur. After you have a record of how you perceive these events, begin to experiment by changing one thing at a time. Then observe how it affects the others.

As scientists our powers of observation are invaluable to us. The above exercise requires you to sharpen those skills. Most of us are so immune to our environment that we hardly notice our spouse in the morning when awakening. As a singer you can't expect to sing about something unless you're excited by it. After all, singing stems from a heightened sense of reality. When we are truly excited about an experience, we are moved to sing about it, or at the very least, moan, cry, or yell about it.

The first thing we must know, however, if we are going to sing well is how our "machinery" works. A mechanic who customarily works on Ford trucks wouldn't do too well repairing a Mercedes sports car. Know your instrument. And since you are your instrument, learn how your body and your voice work. Basically, the mechanics of the voice go something like this:

1. Something stimulates you to take a breath to speak and/or sing.
2. A message is sent to the brain.
3. You inhale.
4. Air is taken in through the nose and mouth into the lungs.
5. The lungs expand, the diaphragm (a muscle located beneath the ribs) descends, pushing the lower abdomen out and down.
6. At the same time the intercostal back muscles (the muscles between your ribs) expand, pushing out across your back.
7. An air pressure system is created by the elastic nature of the involved muscles and you experience a desire to let the breath go soon after it is taken in.
8. The breath is released and sent through soft tissue called

the vocal folds, resembling a disc perforated by small holes through which air jets blow in rapid succession.

9. The breath sets off motion between the vocal folds, which produce an initial set of vibrations.

10. The vibrations, depending upon their speed, will re-sound (or resonate) in different locations in the body—e.g. sinus cavities, skull, etc.

11. Initial and secondary vibrations sound until the breath ceases or they are deliberately stopped—e.g. swallowing, closing one's mouth.

This is, of course, an oversimplification of how the voice functions, but it shall serve as a guide for our further work. What's important is that you should have some clear idea of how the "machinery" works, before you get "under the hood." For our learning purposes, I will separate the act of singing into two cat-egories so that we can examine each more closely. They are: *breath* and *sound*.

Below are diagrams of how the body works as you breathe.

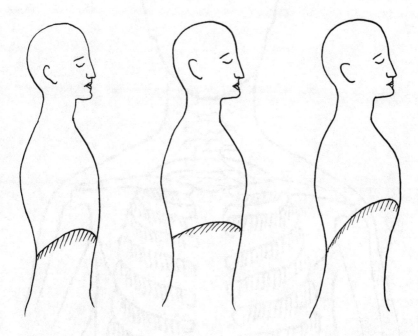

The diaphragm during its three states: at rest, during inhalation, and during exhalation.

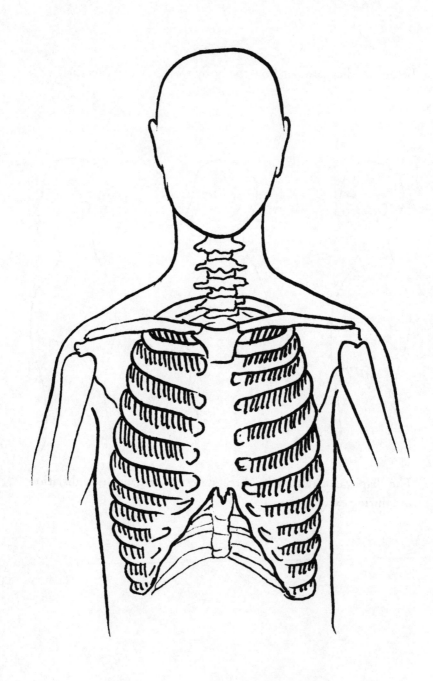

Diagram of the Intercostal Muscles

Inhale now and place your hands and arms on your ribs. Feel them expand like an accordion. These are your intercostal back muscles at work. Every breath will push them out as if you were pulling on opposite ends of a rubber band, as in the following diagram:

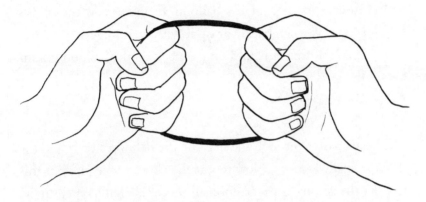

The effect of the breath during inhalation on the intercostal back muscles can be compared to stretching a rubber band with both hands pulling in opposite directions.

The Concept of Constructive Tension

The "elastic" quality of the muscles helps to give your breath and sound "energy." As you breathe, notice that when you inhale there is a feeling of wanting to let the breath go almost immediately upon taking it in. This creates a surface tension in the body. Not a destructive tension that will inhibit vibration, but a *constructive tension* which will help to enhance sound.

The way in which constructive tension helps us sing is by maintaining the expansion the breath makes and supplying the breath with momentum when you release it. You are helping to conserve breath as you sing by letting it go slowly. Try this:

1. Blow air into a balloon.
2. Hold the neck of the balloon tightly after you finish filling it with air.
3. Observe the skin of the balloon. Examine how the skin is so tight you can hardly grasp it with your fingers.
4. Then release your hold on the neck of the balloon gradually.
5. What happens?

The air passes through the neck of the balloon slowly and the skin gradually loosens. Now repeat the above procedure but this time let the air out of the balloon all at once. What happens now?

The balloon flies out of your hand very quickly. Why? By keeping the air contained inside the balloon, it gathers energy. When you allow the air to pass slowly through the neck of the balloon, the small amount of air is propelled out of the balloon with larger amounts of "energy." When you let the air out of the balloon quickly or all at once the energy is used immediately and dissipates quickly. In other words, the elastic energy created by the air stretching the balloon is converted into kinetic energy when the air is released.

Your voice behaves in similar ways. When you inhale and open your mouth to sing or speak, your voice reflects the amount of energy inherent in the breath. Meaning, when you sing you must slow down the release of breath in order to sustain pitch and maintain the power of the voice.

Experiment with this concept by standing comfortably with your hands on each side of your waist and have your index and middle finger touching each other. Then take a breath in and feel your waist expand, much like the balloon did when you filled it with air. Your middle and index fingers on each hand should be at least an inch apart. Now release the air and feel your waist retract, resembling the empty balloon. Your fingers should be touching again. Try this a few times until you feel as if this type of breathing becomes natural to you. This is what we refer to as *diaphragmatic breathing.* The incoming breath depresses the diaphragm and pushes the abdomen out while it pushes the lower intestines down, both making room for "energized" breath. (See the following diagram.)

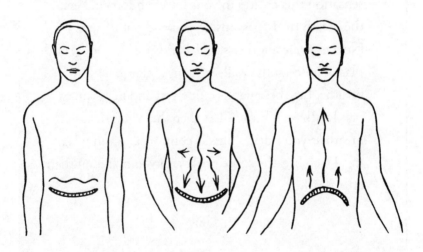

The diaphragm at rest. The breath is calm.

The diaphragm pushed down by inhalation. The breath is stored and becomes energized.

The diaphragm rising during exhalation. The breath is released with energy.

VISUALIZATION EXERCISE FOR
DEVELOPING CONSTRUCTIVE TENSION

1. Stand erect but at ease with legs apart. Close your eyes. Feel your hands get heavy and pull down toward the floor. Feel your head lightly resting on your neck. Imagine it being held straight by little strings dangling from the ceiling. Feel a space between your head and neck. Feel your neck get long. You are now very tall and relaxed and breathing freely.

2. Now bring your awareness to your abdomen. Feel the breath enter you and leave you while focusing on the sensation this creates in your lower abdomen. Feel the breath freely pass inside you and out of you. Now imagine another set of hands inside you, gently placed holding the walls of your abdomen. Now breathe. Let these hands guide you and help you expand with each breath. Let them help you sustain the breath as you exhale. This is comfortable and relaxing. Deep breaths come easily and you maintain them effortlessly.

Locating Points of Constructive Tension in the Body

The major processes of the diaphragm and its control are involuntary. The idea of controlling the involuntary muscles may at first seem impossible; and it is, if we use the same methods as with the voluntary muscles: compulsion.

How then shall we control the involuntary muscles? By *using our imagination.* By using our minds and emotions, we can acquire genuine reactions from muscles, which are beyond our ability to consciously control. For example: Imagine you see a good friend of yours about to cross the street. He is looking the wrong way and doesn't see the truck coming. He steps off the curb and is in direct line with the truck. In one coordinated action you:

1. become energized and determined to stop him from crossing the street.
2. move forward as if to physically stop him.
3. drop your jaw (loosely).
4. gasp. Your lungs fill with air.
5. hold your breath until it bursts forth in a shout.
6. call to him loudly, "Watch out—There's a truck coming."

When we sing, we must use our imaginations as in the above exercise. We must refuse to use our voices in a nonchalant fashion. Sure it would be easy. It would require less effort. When we sing, however, we must have direction and purpose. We must be energized. Then and only then can we expect to maintain tone and pitch. Remember, singing reflects a sense of heightened reality. A sense of heightened reality means having an acute aware-

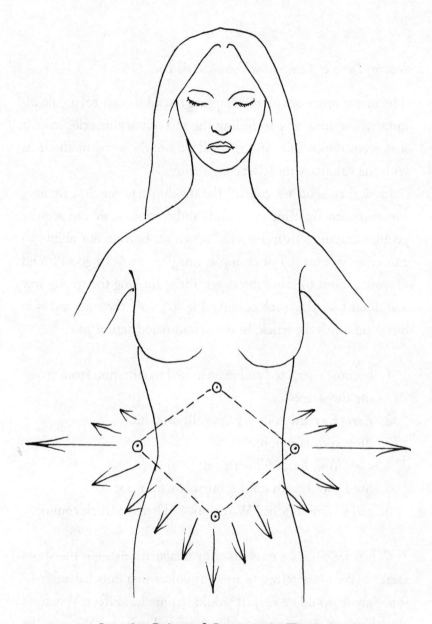

Locating Points of Constructive Tension

At which points in your body do you experience a "tightness" or "pulling sensation" during and after inhalation? Compare your observations with the points marked on this drawing.

ness of things and people around you as well as being sensitive to what's happening within yourself. In the above exercise you practiced using your imagination while observing how your emotional reaction influenced your body. The next exercise will further develop your imagination and again demonstrate how the mind affects the body.

EXERCISE FOR THE IMAGINATION

For this exercise, stand comfortably, with your arms relaxed by your side. Close your eyes, take a couple of comfortable breaths. Then start.

1. You're standing waiting for the bus and a childhood friend, whom you have not seen in ten years, is on line with you. You greet her: "I can't believe it! Is that _____ ? How are you?"
2. You've just had an argument with your significant other. He/she suggests a walk outside. You reply, "Leave me alone."
3. Repeat the above exercise, only this time you are not angry with your significant other. This time communicate love.

Be aware of what and how you're feeling. There should obviously be a distinct difference in physicality, energy, and emotion with all three examples. Explore how the difference manifests itself in your voice. Make note of volume, clarity, and tension in the muscles. Then try it again.

Realize that as a singer, you are drawing on your natural abilities. We are all capable of singing from a heightened state if we remember that emotion equals energy. When you allow yourself to emote without reservation, you allow all your body's energy to surface. As your energy surfaces, it becomes available to fuel your breath which in turn will support sound with the pressure it creates. This is much like an airplane as it begins to leave the ground. When the plane takes off, there exists a gravitational pull downward while the plane creates an opposing force to go up. What results is a tension between the ground and the plane. If the force pulling the plane down were equal to the force pushing the plane up, the plane would merely be suspended in air. (This happens when the plane finds a cruising altitude and reduces its speed so as to stabilize the ascent.) During takeoff, however, the push up must overpower the gravitational pull downward. When you sing, you must act like the plane in takeoff and break through the "gravity barrier." You must create breath so fueled with energy that it will be able to sustain a full spectrum of sound. Understanding this, are you aware of where your body's natural "gravitational pull" is located?

Finding Your Center of Gravity

Each one of us walks with an unconscious connection to a "center" in our body which governs the way we move. Some of us may

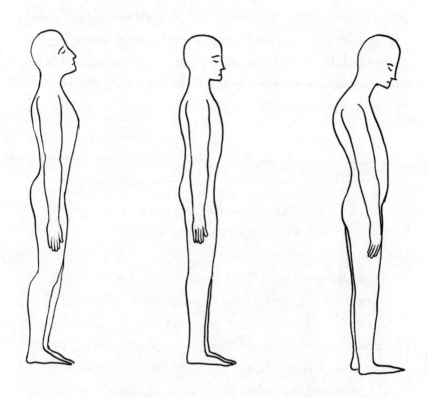

Finding Your Center of Gravity

High Center—Feeling the "pull" up in your chest area will lead you to walk with stiff shoulders and an arched back. Your breathing will be shallow.

Low Center—Feeling a low center of gravity will guide you toward better breathing by leaving you room to sense your diaphragm and intercostal muscles and by leaving the chest clear for resonation.

A weak posture is where you walk round-shouldered and feel a gravitational pull downward from the chest. This makes breathing labored, leaves you feeling tired, and creates little room for breath expansion or resonation.

feel grounded by our abdomens, some by our shoulders, some by our faces or heads, and some by our pelvis, chest, or rib cage. By identifying the part of our bodies that grounds us and by acknowledging its influence on our posture and movement, we can begin to understand the flow of our own breath along with understanding what we must do in order to maximize our breath capacity. The exercise below is especially designed to help you do this.

EXERCISE FOR FINDING
YOUR CENTER OF GRAVITY

First relax your body. Stretch your arms up and out from your sides. Then gently roll down to touch your toes and slowly uncurl yourself, bringing your hands to your sides as you bring your head to an upright position. Tense your toes. Release them. Tense your hands. Release them. Tighten your buttocks and release them. Tense your face and then release it. Take a couple of long relaxed breaths. Now:

1. Walk across the room in full view of a mirror.
2. Examine the motion of your walk and the posture of your body.
3. Which part of your body is leading?

Once you have decided which part of your body is leading when you walk, your center of gravity should become clear to you. If you are leading with your rib cage, you are breathing a little high. If you are leading with your hips or pelvis, you probably have a good idea where your most powerful breath is.

For example, I used to walk leading from my upper abdomen, slightly below my rib cage. At times I would arch my back and lose touch with my lower abdomen, hips, and buttocks. In effect, what this was doing to my breathing was cutting it off from its most powerful source—the diaphragm. We can then see how my singing would suffer if I did not work on adjusting this.

Realize that it might take you a few times doing this exercise until any awareness becomes noticeable. Most of us have little knowledge of how we move and are not aware of the tensions we carry and where we carry them.

EXERCISE FOR BREATHING
THROUGH YOUR CENTER OF GRAVITY

Once you feel comfortable with your center of gravity, try breathing from that point. Try panting in an uneven pattern to awaken those parts of your body that don't feel energized. Below is a suggestion for breathing patterns. (For our purposes long breaths shall be held to the count of five and short breaths to the count of two.)

1. Inhale: Short, Short, Long
   Exhale: Short, Short, Long
2. Inhale: Long
   Exhale: Short, Short, Short, Short, Long

Creating a Pressure System

When you sing, you learn about the importance of breaking through the "gravity barrier." This means the breath must be steady and fast for higher notes, slower and steady for lower notes. The higher the tone, the faster the breath. The lower the tone, the slower the breath and the more relaxed you need to be. To examine the effects of an air-pressure system, try the following experiment.

Float a Ping-Pong ball on the draft from a hair dryer. The ball always sits right in the middle. This is an example of what's called the Bernoulli effect. Bernoulli observed that whenever air moves, its pressure drops. In fact, the faster air moves, the more pressure drops. The air moves fastest in the center of the jet, so pressure here is low. If the ball ever drifts to one side, it is soon pushed into the middle again by the higher pressure where the air moves more slowly at the edges of the air stream.[1]

Now imagine that the ball is your voice balancing on the stream of air that you produce. Try to keep the "ball" steady on a constant flow of breath. Another way to measure the constant flow of breath is to light a candle, place it in front of you and exhale. Watch the flame. Does it move steadily away from you? Does it flicker? Does it stay still? Record your observations.

---

[1] *How Science Works* by Judith Hann, Reader's Digest Books, Pleasantville, N.Y., 1991, p. 129.

Making Sound

When someone first comes to me to help them sing, we usually start by just making sound the way a baby first makes sound. We babble. "Feel the vibration on your lips," I tell them. Play with it. Does it feel good? A lot of us are much too embarrassed to actually "play" like this, but it is an invaluable way to learn. Go ahead, I say, feel that buzzing sensation in your mouth. Then feel it in your chest. Tap yourself like a drum. Where do you sense most of the vibration coming from? Invariably they tell me their throat. To which I say, "Yes and where else?"

Because while it's true that the source of the vocal tone is the larynx (your voice box), located in the middle part of your neck, we cannot say that the voice as we hear it comes from the larynx. The basic tone is modified and amplified by resonance (re-sounding) after it leaves the larynx, and is shaped into meaningful language by the mouth, tongue, lips, and teeth before we hear it. In other words, although you feel the vibration in your throat there will be a second vibration (a sympathetic vibration set off by the initial vibration) that will sound elsewhere in the body and will give you your voice.

Every object has its own natural frequency. For instance, if allowed to vibrate freely, it always tends to vibrate at the same rate. If you strike a bell, for instance, it will always give the same note. Similarly, the pendulum in an old clock always tends to swing to and fro at the same rate. You can make objects vibrate faster or more slowly than their natural frequency by jogging them at appropriate intervals. This is called forced vibration. But when an object is jogged at just the same rate as its natural frequency, it vibrates in sympathy and the vibrations become much stronger. This is called resonance.

For instance, sing "ah" and place your hand on your chest. Do you feel it vibrate? Sing the same "ah" again and place your hand on your throat. Feel your throat buzz with vibration at the same time your chest is also buzzing. Now sing "ah" in a higher voice and place your hands on and around your face. Where do you feel the vibration? You will find that you will always feel a vibration in your throat area, the origin of sound, as well as feeling a secondary vibration somewhere else in your body, the place where the sound actually lives. (We will work more on finding and placing sound in chapter 6, The Detective.)

Making sound is a highly technical and complicated process. There are many groups of muscles involved and many physical factors that affect your voice. As a scientist, it's important for you to ask the question, "What happens when . . . ?" This approach will always help you look at yourself and your voice in a new way.

For instance, What happens when I hum a low tone and keep my lips together? What happens when I hum a high-pitched tone and keep my lips slightly parted? What happens when I breathe slow and long as opposed to breathing fast and shallow? Treat your body as an instrument and play it. No one knows you better than yourself.

Realize that you are much like a stringed instrument. The sound produced depends on the size of the string and how tightly it is stretched. Your vocal folds are capable of stretching and changing shape so you can make a large variety of sounds. But what makes each of our sounds our own is that our res-

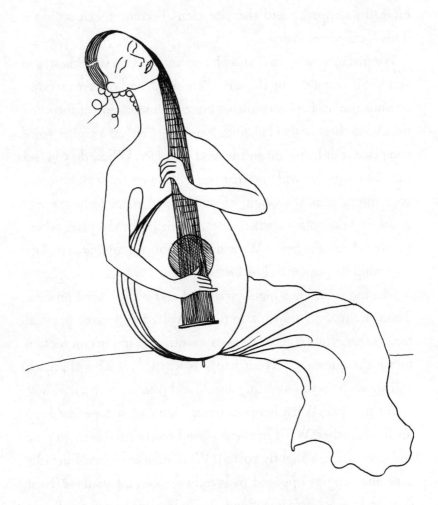

Treat your body as an instrument and play it.

onators (pharynx, soft palate, hard palate, nasal cavities, and larynx) are all different shapes. In other words, the infinite varieties
of these resonators, like the features of a face, give every voice a
unique sound and character.

WARM-UP EXERCISE

Stand comfortably with your feet on the floor and your shoulders relaxed. Take a deep but comfortable breath and let it out. Do this again. Now take the breath again but this time let a long sigh out, starting from high to low. I call this vocal "free-falling." Try this once more, staying relaxed and let your voice fall with your breath gently. Now take the same breath again and start from the bottom and rise upward. You will find that it might be slightly more difficult for you. You will need a bit more energy to glide up than down. Why? Think about climbing a hill as opposed to walking down a hill. Going up you are at odds with the natural gravitational pull down, while stepping down you are following the existing forces. The same principle applies in working your voice. As you travel up into the higher regions of the voice, the sound must "travel" a greater distance in order to be amplified by the face and skull resonators. The lower sounds are amplified by the chest and mouth, so there is not such a great need for the breath to "carry" the sound that far.

Try this sighing exercise again. Stay relaxed and breathe using your diaphragm and intercostal muscles. Make sure your waist is expanding and that you are not lifting your shoulders as you breathe. Now sigh from top to bottom. Pay attention to how you're feeling.

Don't listen too closely to the sound. What's important is how you're feeling. When you are sighing at the top, imagine the sound traveling through you all the way down into your lower abdomen. Give the sound a picture—see it as a waterfall, or see it as maple syrup. In any case, feel and see the sound as it travels. When you feel comfortable with this part of the exercise, start the sigh again, but this time pick a place in between the top and bottom to stop and sustain the sigh. In other words, pick a tone and sing it for a couple of seconds. Hold it. Feel it. Then let it go. You are now beginning to learn to develop your speaking voice and transform it into a singing voice.

Try this exercise a couple of times until you feel at ease with it. It's a wonderful warm-up for anytime you wish to sing.

Working the Song

Now think of that song you chose to work on throughout reading this book. Sing the first couple of lines to yourself. Now sing those lines out loud, with your hands on your waist, making sure you are breathing correctly. Try not to think too much as you do this. Simply observe. It is very beneficial to write your observations down as you make them. For instance, "While I'm singing I notice that I hold my stomach in instead of letting it expand and contract," or "When I reach the high point of the phrase, I notice my throat gets tight and the sound is then hard to make." Before you can get better at something, it's necessary to understand your shortcomings. Know them so you have a clear idea of what it is you need to correct. How will you know how to correct these seeming weak spots? You'll experiment and find what works. Remember, discovery is often accidental. It then becomes necessary that we let go of our conscious objective temporarily so something unexpected can happen. True learning is by no means linear. Let your intuition surface. Then examine your hunches.

How Breath and Sound Affect Each Other

As you begin to develop your voice out of natural sounds made by the body, the more you will connect your breath and your voice and the easier singing (and speaking) will become. Remember to think of your breath as "fuel for the engine" and no matter what—keep it going.

BREATH AND SOUND EXERCISE

Here's a funny exercise to try. All of us have pants somewhere in our closet that are too tight for us. Put them
on. (If you don't have a pair of pants that are too tight, I
congratulate you and instead, pick a belt and buckle it
one notch too tight.) Try to take a deep breath and have

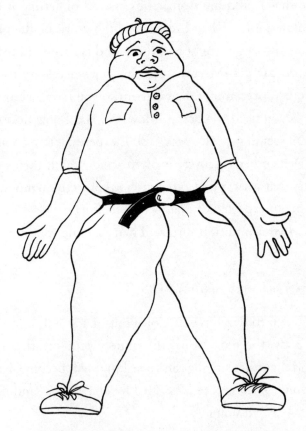

Try to take a deep breath and have your waistline expand with your
belt buckled one notch too tight. How does it feel?

your waist expand. How does it feel? Can you breathe efficiently? Now try to let out some sound. How does that feel? I'm supposing you're pretty uncomfortable at the moment. Without the freedom of having your diaphragm lower, and your lower abdomen dropping, it becomes increasingly difficult to let out sound. Why? You are not taking in enough breath. Nor are you comfortable enough to utilize the breath that you have. Without the proper amount of breath, making sound becomes arduous, if not impossible. Too much pressure is put on the larynx and vocal folds and soon the "engine" will simply burn itself out due to overexertion.

The Articulators
THE TONGUE, JAW, AND LIPS

One of the most important things governing the quality of our voices when we sing or speak is how well we articulate the sounds. How well we shape the sound with our mouths (tongues, lips, and teeth) determines how well we're understood.

THE TONGUE

The tongue is far more important than you suspect. It can shape sound but it can also interfere with the production of sound.

And more often than not it does interfere because it becomes the receptacle of the body's tension.

EXERCISES FOR THE TONGUE

See if you can say this quickly: "Take a ticket, take a ticket, take a ticket Tom."

Do you feel the tip of your tongue touch the front of your mouth, just behind your teeth, then travel to the back of your mouth and touch your hard palate (the roof of your mouth)? Try it again: "Take a ticket, take a ticket, take a ticket Tom."

Try it faster and faster each time. If you can say it rather quickly without too much trouble you are probably not housing too much tension in your tongue. If you feel like this exercise is difficult and are finding it hard to pronounce the words and be understood, you can guess that there's probably too much tension in your tongue.

Now try: "Ya ya ya ya ya ya ya ya ya." Do this without moving your jaw. Just move your tongue. If you feel like this is simple and your jaw remains still while you sing or speak these syllables, your tongue is facile. If, on the other hand your jaw moves as you say each "ya," you can bet there is some relaxation work that remains to be done. (Exercises for the mouth and tongue are supplied at the end of this chapter.)

The height of the tongue in the mouth varies the resonance of the vocal tone. In other words, where you place your tongue in your mouth has a great effect on how you sound. As a part of the tongue is lifted high toward the hard palate, it creates a narrow connecting passageway between the cavities behind and in front of that point. If the tongue is lowered, the connecting passageway between the cavities grows more open. To observe how the height of the tongue affects vowel production, compare the vowels in feed, fade, and fad.[2]

In the long "e" sound of feed, the tongue is curled up at either side pressed up against the molars. In the long "a" sound of fade (a combination sound), the tongue lies mostly flat at the bottom of the mouth and then curls up against the molars once again toward the second part of the vowel sound (feh-ee-d). The short "a" sound of fad requires the tongue to lie flat in the mouth. Experiment with all five vowel sounds and see if you can decipher the shape of your tongue during each.

The five vowel sounds in singing are: "ah, eh, ee, oh, oo."

Following is a diagram showing the face and mouth with the articulators marked. Observe the tongue in relation to the oral cavity.

[2]*Improving Voice and Articulation* by Hilda Fisher, Houghton Mifflin Company, Boston, 1955, p. 213.

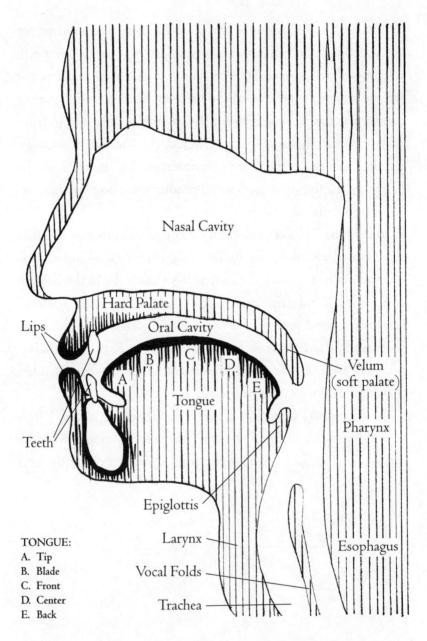

Nasal Cavity

Hard Palate

Lips

Oral Cavity

B   C

A   D

E

Tongue

Velum
(soft palate)

Teeth

Pharynx

Epiglottis

Larynx

Esophagus

Vocal Folds

Trachea

TONGUE:
A. Tip
B. Blade
C. Front
D. Center
E. Back

This is your face and mouth with the articulators marked: the lips, teeth, tongue (a. tip, b. blade, c. front, d. center, e. back), the lower jaw, the soft palate.

EXERCISES FOR THE BACK OF THE TONGUE

Now say "ng-gah." Say it again. "ng-gah." Where does
your tongue rest in your mouth as you say this? It should
be changing position with each syllable. As you say "ng,"
your tongue should be high up against your hard palate.
When you say "gah" your tongue should lower and leave
a round open space at the back of your throat. Try this
in front of a mirror. Say "ng-gah" and watch what
happens. Now try letting a tone out on these syllables.
Watch what happens to the sound. When you say "ng,"
the sound should stop and resemble a hum. When you
say "gah" it should really open up and sing.

It's as if you are stopping the flow of water. You are creating a
natural stopgap with your tongue.

When you remove this stopgap, you are allowing the sound to
"flow." If there is tension in the tongue, however, you are somewhat restricted in how you maneuver it.

Try saying this: "Googilee oogilee googilee oogilee
googilee oogilee gah." Repeat: "Googilee oogilee
googilee oogilee googilee oogilee gah."

What are your observations? Was this easy to say? Did your tongue get stuck? If it did, at what point did it start to slow down? Do this exercise a few times. Make sure you are aware of what is happening in your mouth. Write down anything that comes to mind concerning the process. You never know what is going to be a valuable insight later.

Try this exercise daily and see what happens. Does it become easier? Are you a little more sure of what's "supposed" to happen? Enter your daily observations and begin to look for some changes in how you shape sound with your tongue.

THE JAW

The lower jaw is an important articulator. It is used to help us pronounce words like apple, opposite, octave, and octopus. It opens and closes voluntarily and gives us much freedom of speech and expression. It also doubles as a resonator. Its hard, bony surface is great for the re-sounding of vibration. Unless, of course, you are harboring some tension in your jaw as most of us do—some of us more than others. I hate to point a finger, but there's a group of us out there who have enormous trouble letting go of our jaws. Those of you who have either experienced this firsthand or know someone who has to deal with this understand. These folks talk as though their mouths are wired shut. The tongue is working fine, they're pronouncing all of their words, but their jaw doesn't move. It's locked.

EXERCISE FOR THE JAW

Try saying this: "Apples and oranges are always my favorite fruit. Apples and oranges are always my favorite fruit."

Now put one hand under your chin and repeat the phrase. Does your chin lower? This time place the index finger of both hands on either side of your jaw (about a half inch down from your ears) and repeat "Apples and oranges are always my favorite fruit." What do you feel? Does your jaw lower? How free does it feel? Does it feel tight? Is it painful to lower it?

What makes the jaw temperamental is the muscle that attaches it to the skull: the temporalis muscle. Sometimes when you are anxious or upset you might clench your jaw or grind your teeth. This causes the muscle to shorten and be less flexible. There is a condition commonly referred to as temperomandibular joint dysfunction (TMJ), which is a chronic tension in the jaw muscles, which then will inhibit movement. In very severe cases, movement might be restricted altogether. Now say: "Yah-ki-tee-yah-ki-tee-yah-ki-tee-yah. Yah-ki-tee-yah-ki-tee-yah-ki-tee-yah."

Ideally you want your jaw muscles to be relaxed so they are free to move. If, however, you are tensing these muscles you must work on releasing them or they will prevent you from making sound the way you need to in order to sing. To relax these muscles, try this exercise: "Humm-mah, humm-mah, humm-mah." Say this slowly and softly to yourself a few times. Gradually work on releasing the jaw as you say the "mah" until you can actually feel a tiny buzz in your lower jaw. You must concentrate and let go of any distractions. Pay attention to how the sensation changes. Remember: tension inhibits vibration.

Another reason your jaw may be tense is hidden anger. You will find that we accumulate a lot of "stuff" we don't want to deal with and house it somewhere in the body. The jaw and tongue are ready recipients for these unwanted emotions. Conveniently the anger is stored and we forget that it is there. That is, until we try to express ourselves and something prevents us from doing so in the manner that we wish. That something is an uncooperative jaw and tongue.

I currently have a student who is a joyful person. She is bright, highly motivated, energetic, and talented. Yet there remains one stumbling block in our study together. Her jaw is so tight she has trouble connecting her words and her tongue is consistently in the wrong place in her mouth at the wrong time. Is it anger? Is it tension? I haven't yet deduced. But even without knowing why, there is still something I can do to help. What do I do to help? Make her aware of the problem and support her in gently trying to remedy it. We practice relaxation exercises and exercise the muscles. We do visualization exercises and we talk about her life—What's going on, how she's feeling, what's new at school and at home, etc. By keeping her relaxed during a lesson, I have a better chance at having her relax when she sings. She is aware of the problem and is experimenting with different solutions. I remind her that she is her own instrument and that the teacher

is simply a guide and witness. I tell her *find your own answers.*
They will always serve you better than trusting someone else's
judgment.

THE LIPS

Lips are great things. They help us speak. They look fabulous and
they're great for kissing. They're also really important helpers in
singing. Think about that old favorite tongue twister "Peter
Piper picked a peck of pickled peppers." You couldn't say it without your lips, and you couldn't sing the Beach Boys' "Barbra
Ann" either. Life just wouldn't be the same. How do we use the
lips efficiently? Easy. Wake them up every day. Razz a lot. Blow
air through your lips.

EXERCISE FOR THE LIPS

Say: "Butter, baby, butter, baby, butter, baby boy." Or,
"Mary and Mom made a maple malted." Or, "Polly
picks pansies perfectly."

You get the idea. Anything that brings the top and bottom lips
together will help you exercise the lips and keep them alive and
energized. The lips are not as problematic as the jaw and tongue
as they don't usually house too much tension. What you do have
to guard against, however, is an unwilling mouth. Meaning, all of
us tend to get lazy with our pronunciation at times. Our lips become slow and sluggish. We slur our words. By waking our lips

up every day you have a better chance of singing and/or speaking clearly. Each of us needs to be heard and understood. Better diction yields better communication. Better communication makes for a happier life.

The lips are also used in pronouncing the consonant "w," either at the beginning of words (willow) or at the end of words (how).

ADDITIONAL EXERCISES FOR THE LIPS

Try saying: "Willows wait to be watered." Or, "Why won't we?" Now place your hands on your mouth and repeat one or both phrases. Do you feel a gathering at the lips, a kind of coming together at the center of your mouth? This is the shape of the consonant "w" before or after a word.

Try: "How now brown cow." Notice the same formation of the lips. Do these a few times until you become aware of moving the lips in this manner. Remind yourself daily and make up fun sayings for yourself to say. Add a tune to make the exercise enjoyable.

I want to make it clear that I have given you simply an introduction to improving your diction. One could write volumes on phonetics and the physiology of the voice. Our goal here is to explore how we make sound and what is necessary to do so.

Now once again, bring your attention to that song on page 42 that you have chosen to work on. Let's start at the middle this time. Close your eyes. Try to relax and sing. Notice some of the things we have been discussing. For instance, your mouth. How does the sound feel in your mouth? Are you aware of the shapes you use in order to sing it? How about your tongue? Does it feel tight? Do you feel the back of your throat is open and unobstucted? What about your jaw? Are you aware of any movement? Is it relaxed?

It will be a while until you become aquainted with all aspects of your body while singing in order to answer these questions quickly and definitively. Take your time. Experiment enough so that these unfamiliar aspects of voice production become routine. What's best is to remember to do these experiments and exercises in the true spirit of the scientist. Yearn to learn.

In your pursuit of knowledge, I can wish you nothing better than the uplift in spirit that flows from perceiving the beauty inherent in the process of breathing and making sound.

ARTICULATION EXERCISES

1 | **Tongue Touching Teeth:**

Continue up by 1/2 steps.

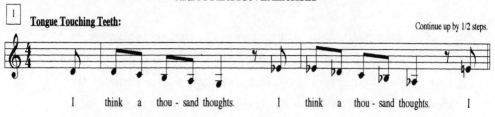

I   think   a   thou - sand thoughts.   I   think   a   thou - sand thoughts.   I

2 | **Tongue touching teeth ridge:**

Continue up by 1/2 steps.

Nev - er   not   now.   Nev - er   not   now.   Nev - er   not   now.

3 | **Tip of tongue:**

Continue up by 1/2 steps.

Lah Leh Lee Loh Loo(u)   Lah Leh Lee Loh Loo(u)

4 | **Tongue touching teeth ridge, hard palate and both lips:**

Continue up by 1/2 steps.

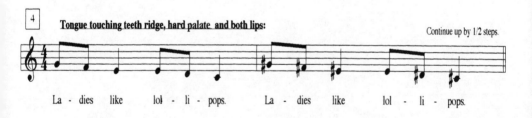

La - dies like lol - li - pops.   La - dies like lol - li - pops.

5 | **Throat and both lips:**

Continue up by 1/2 steps.

Hap - py, hap - py Me.   Hap - py, hap - py Me.   Hap - py, hap - py Me.

7 **For both lips:** (Repeat 4-bar pattern up a 1/2 step.)

Ba Ba Ba Umm Ba   Ba Ba Ba Umm Ba   Ba Ba Ba Umm Ba   Ba Ba Ba Ba

8 **Lower lip and upper teeth:**

We   vis - it - ed   a   val - ley   and   a   vine - yard.   We   vis - it - ed   a   val - ley   and   a   vine - yard.   We

vis - it - ed   a   val - ley   yes,   we   vis - it - ed   a   val - ley.   Yes,   we   vis - it - ed   a   val - ley   and   a   vine - yard.

9 **Tongue touching teeth ridge and the hard palate:** Continue up by 1/2 steps.

Take   a   tick - et,   Tom.   Take   a   tick - et,   Tom.

11 **Both lips:** Continue up by 1/2 steps.   **12** **Both lips:** Continue up by 1/2 steps.

Wil - lows wait   to   be   wat - ered.   Wil - lows wait   to   be   wat - ered.   Why won't we?   Why won't we?

THE DETECTIVE

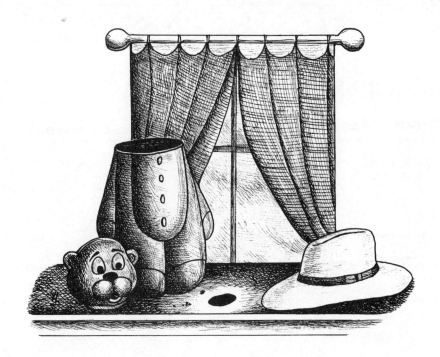

CHAPTER SIX

THE DETECTIVE

"The truth lies before you in disguise."

I t was dark and quiet in the house that Thursday night. Friday morning, really. Everyone had gone to bed. Everyone, except Mara. She was still bent over her desk, busy writing, desperately trying to meet this week's newspaper deadline. When she finally did, at 2 A.M., she tiptoed into the kitchen and switched on the overhead light above the sink. The counter was crowded with boxes and bags filled with treats and goodies she had received from the family for her birthday, but didn't have time to eat. They were all there waiting for her, tightly wrapped in their bakery containers. Still, Mara couldn't help noticing that something was wrong. In the soft light she could see a trail of crumbs beside one of the packages. She glanced at the boxes tied with string, then back to the counter. Had someone been there before her? Had the boxes already been opened?

She stepped out of the kitchen and peered around the corner into the bathroom. It was empty. She checked the living room—everything looked serene. Just at that moment, she heard something. It sounded like footsteps and the crumpling of an empty paper bag just before you get ready to throw it away. She spun around quickly and caught a glimpse of what seemed like a shadow. In an instant the shadow was gone, too quick to catch. Mara couldn't help feeling the shadow had a familiar frame and yet remained unidentifiable. She gasped quietly to herself, all the time wondering who it could be. There was no other sound. Then she noticed a brown paper bag lying by her foot. Was this the cause of the sound she heard minutes before? Did the shadow drop it on its way? Or did she step on it herself and not notice? Plagued with questions, she stood in the hallway at the top of the stairs.

Just to eliminate the suspects, she went to check on her husband and daughter. Both were still in their beds, sound asleep. She ran to the front door and checked the locks. All were securely fastened. The shadow had disappeared. All was again quiet, except for her suspicion. She reentered the kitchen, determined to get to the bottom of the situation. She walked over to the food-laden counter. She untied the plastic bag. She released the flaps of the cardboard box and opened it. Could she tell whether someone else had already eaten from it? Yes. Cookies were bitten into and quite a few were definitely missing. "But who took them?" she wondered. "And when?" She was baffled.

Catching the time on the kitchen clock wall, she remembered

her morning deadline and her need for sleep. Resolved to investigate the matter further the next day, she left the kitchen for the bathroom to wash up and brush her teeth. In front of her lay another clue. There on the edge of the sink rested her toothbrush, bristles damp, as if someone had just used it. Aha! Someone *had* been there before! "But who?" she wondered.

Mara gazed into the mirror on the bathroom cabinet. "Who?" she wondered, "Who?" Then in an instant, the answer appeared staring her in the face. There in the mirror, she saw the faint film of a milk mustache and the telltale sign of cookie crumbs in the creases of her mouth and on her cheeks. "Me? It was me!?" she cried. It all quickly became clear. So preoccupied and weary, working away at her desk, she never remembered getting up for that break, walking into the kitchen, sampling the cookies and drinking the milk. She didn't even connect that it was she who crumpled the brown paper bag. Her body may have entered the kitchen but her mind never left the desk. Mara laughed quietly to herself, then brushed her teeth and headed for bed. The case of the missing cookies had finally been solved.

Being a Detective in Your Own Life

How often do we hide things from ourselves? How often do we not realize where we left the house keys or our wallet or the notes for that morning's report? How often do we conveniently forget that we are upset, lonely, or angry and distract ourselves with another activity? How often are we just plain absentminded?

I would think that most of us, if we are living productive lives, have periodic lapses but are generally responsible to ourselves and those close to us. However, the point I'm raising here has more to do with how we are to treat the problem when it arises—in life and in singing.

In being a detective in your own life, you have to start by knowing what it is you are doing and when and why you are doing it at any given moment. This means, you must be conscious. You have to be present. Otherwise, you run the risk of functioning on automatic pilot. Automatic pilot is okay if you want to cook the same way you read a book. Or run a mile the same way you type a paper. Or make love the same way you ride the subway to work. In life, each activity requires your separate and full attention. And in giving your full attention, you will most likely follow suit by feeling the need to make choices. By making choices you are deciding what your life will be from one day to the next, from one moment to the next. This in turn will give your life a shape, a design, a purpose. By making choices, you assume responsibility for your life. By assuming responsibility you are guaranteed a more satisfying life by the mere fact that no one but you is at the helm running the ship according to your own wants and needs, your own dreams and desires. What could be better?

You'd be surprised. Given the opportunity, a lot of us shy away from making these decisions for ourselves. Why? I'm sure there are lots of reasons, but perhaps the most common one is we'd rather have someone or something to blame for our unhappiness, our loneliness, our pain, or our misfortune. Conversely, when things go well, we'd rather attribute our good fortune to luck, the stars, our lover, or good genes. It seems we make very few things our responsibility. This is a mistake. The more power we give away or "lose," the more we remain hostage to others and our own unconscious. This poses many problems. But the most dangerous one is not living an authentic life. A life built on and by your own wishes, likes, and dislikes is a life destined for happiness and success. A life that's lived according to someone else's desires and edicts is destined for misery, conflict, and failure. Plain and simple: In order to truly be happy in your life, you must be aware, conscious, and responsible.

The same is true for your life as a singer. Without taking responsibility for yourself and investigating where and what your strengths and problems are, you simply have to take someone else's word for it. I have one word for you: *don't!* Don't think someone else has the answers. Don't believe someone else just because they claim to be an authority.

Making Choices

Recall an incident in your life where you were aware of taking someone else's advice over your own, all the while knowing the advice didn't seem appropriate. We've all listened to someone besides ourselves at one point or another. Remember how you felt. Now think about the outcome. Did things work out as you would have liked? Did they somehow fall short of what you might have wanted?

Write the incident down and imagine a different outcome. One where you listen to yourself and trust your own feelings. Be sure to write a detailed account and examine how you feel as you rewrite the ending to this story. Keep it with you in this book as an example of how you can make choices for yourself. Remember, your choices help to define you and will help you know yourself better.

Every voice is different. Every life is its own. Learn all you can. Ask yourself questions. Investigate. Look for clues. Gather the evidence. Draw your own conclusions. Your voice and your life at times will seem mysterious. But it's *your voice* and *your life.* So *you* take care of it. This is your *only* choice.

As a singer, the detective is invaluable as far as solving certain vocal problems, specifically: voice placement, resonance, and range. First, let's take a look at what voice placement is.

All through college, I studied voice and was constantly supplied with terminology that wasn't very well defined. And if the terms were well defined, their practical applications eluded me. It wasn't until I read Stanislavski's *Building a Character* that I understood. He says, "If you are looking for something, don't go sit on the seashore and expect it to come and find you; you must search, search, search with all the stubbornness in you!"[1] Voice placement is all about finding and feeling the sound vibrate in a certain area in your face and body and remembering where that place is for each note. And because placing a voice refers to the all important resonators that vary in shape and size in every person, there becomes an infinite diversity of tone that each singing voice possesses. In other words, your body is filled with both hard, bony surfaces and open cavities that help each sound to re-sound. So, although the sound might be originating in your voice box, it finds sympathetic vibrations in your sinus cavity, which gives the vibration its specific tone and color. And because each one of us is shaped differently, each of our voices sounds different as well. Therefore you might see yourself as an instrument where each sound is housed in a different place. It is your job as the detective to find where your sounds live. Investigate!

[1] *Building a Character* by Constantin Stanilslavski, Methuen Theatre Arts Books, New York, N.Y., 1949, p. 95.

SOUND-PLACEMENT EXERCISE 1

SOUND-PLACEMENT EXERCISE 1
The Body as Instrument

In order to help yourself find these sounds, you might consider seeing yourself as an instrument like a guitar.

1. Imagine the neck of the guitar inside you. Each note runs up and down the neck of the guitar, also referred to as the fret board. (Keep in mind that on a guitar, the notes get higher as you go down toward the body of the instrument. Your voice works in the opposite way, getting higher as you travel up toward your head.)

2. Close your eyes and sound a low, hearty sound, much like your warrior sound. Feel that sound vibrate somewhere around your solar plexus. Let the sound travel up and try to follow the sound with your mind's eye and see it move along your internal sound board. Follow the vibration with your hand as well and remember where you feel each note.

3. Experiment with very low sounds traveling to very high sounds. Then switch. Know that the very low sounds will vibrate in your chest and throat area while very high sounds will ring somewhere at the top of your head.

4. Start with the sounds at the top of your head and let them roll down. Make sure to visualize the sound as well as feel it. It's very helpful to have some visual aid to establish accurate voice placement.

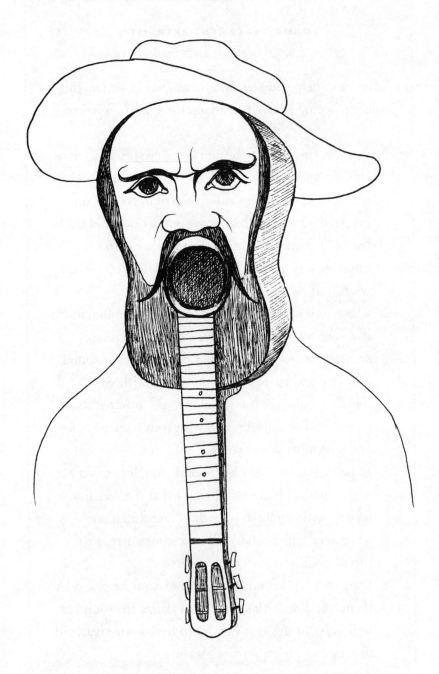

Which instrument are you? Find where your sounds live.

Place all your sounds in the appropriate places in the drawing of the body on page 110. Use it as a guide anytime you sing. It will help you remember where your voice lives. Think of it as your personal road map to your own instrument.

Where are your sounds? Place them like points on a graph. Remember, you and your voice are unique. Only you can find your notes. Let your sensory awareness guide you.

Now try the exercise again.

1. Close your eyes. Allow your warrior sound to emerge. This sound should be low and comfortable. Place it with your mind's eye. Is it in your chest? Do you feel it in your neck and throat?
2. Stay relaxed and keep the breath fueled with energy.
3. Now raise the pitch. Follow the sound as it travels. This time imagine the sound hitting the soundboard and bouncing off. Feel yourself vibrate and re-sound. If you can't feel it right away, don't worry. Try again. You are beginning to sensitize yourself to vibration and resonation. Be patient.

The following drawing is a reference guide to help you place your own sound. Feel free to make drawings yourself. Anything you can do to help yourself is valuable.

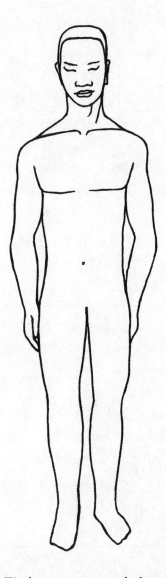

Placing Vibration: Find your notes and then place them on this representation of the body like points on a graph.

Once you've completed placing sound in your body, try the next exercise:

SOUND-PLACEMENT EXERCISE 2
Discovering Your Middle Register

1. Relax your mind and body the best you can.
2. Close your eyes and concentrate on your breathing.
3. Imagine the flow of breath as it passes through you.
4. Feel the natural rise and fall of your abdomen made by the breath.
5. Feel the lungs fill with air.
6. Feel yourself release the air and let it pass through your lips so you can hear it.
7. Now take a breath and release it with sound.
8. Keep your lips closed and let the sound out on "mmm."
9. The sound should be a middle register note, resonating somewhere in or close to your mouth.
10. Feel the vibration.
11. Focus on where the vibration lives in you.
12. When you have an idea of where the vibration lives, open the "mmm" to "mmmah."
13. Keep your awareness on the vibration.
14. Does it change its location once you open your mouth?
15. If it moved, where did it move to?
16. If it stayed in the same place, how was it making the transition from closed mouth to open?

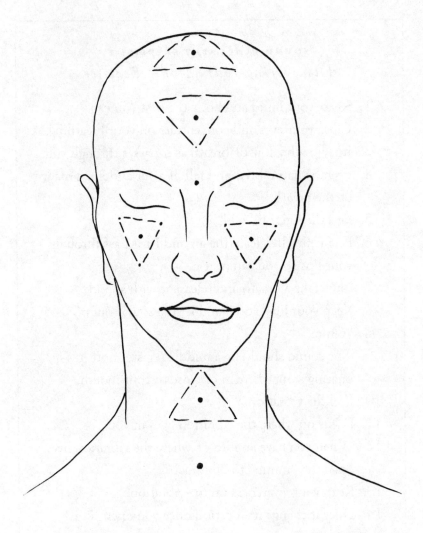

Voice Placement Recognition: Compare this sample representation with your own. How are they alike? How are they different?

Try to be precise. As you hone your voice placement skills, employ your detective and keep a close watch on where or when the resonating note begins to slip away from its home base. If you are not vigilant, you might place all notes in the chest, or all notes in the mask (the front of your face). Either way, remember each sound has its own space. Don't force them all into one "room."

Take into consideration a statement made by Stanislavski on investigating voice placement in his book, *Building a Character:* "I began to explore my head for new reverberant surfaces at every point of my hard palate, soft palate, the top and even the back of my head, . . . and everywhere I found new sounding boards. Each one contributed in some degree or other and added new colorings to enhance the tone."[2]

Let yourself explore the range of sound that you are capable of making. I think you'll be surprised at how much sound lives inside you. Nurture it. Enjoy the sensations. Investigate your instrument.

Now let's repeat that exercise so we can search for the notes living in our lower register.

[2]*Building a Character* by Constantin Stanislavski, Methuen Theatre Arts Books, New York, N.Y., 1949, p. 97.

SOUND-PLACEMENT EXERCISE 3
Discovering Your Lower Register

1. Relax your mind and body the best you can.
2. Close your eyes and concentrate on your breathing.
3. Imagine the flow of breath as it passes through you.
4. Feel the natural rise and fall of your abdomen made by the breath.
5. Feel the lungs fill with air.
6. Feel yourself release the air and let it pass through your lips so you can hear it.
7. Now take a breath and release it with sound.
8. Keep your lips closed and let the sound out on "mmm."
9. The sound should be a lower register note, resonating somewhere in or close to your chest.
10. Feel the vibration.
11. Focus on where the vibration lives in you. (Try to be precise.)
12. When you have an idea of where the vibration lives, open the "mmm" to "mmmuh." Now tap on your chest like a drum.
13. Keep your awareness on the vibration.
14. Does it change its location, once you open your mouth?
15. If it moved, where did it move to?
16. If it stayed, how was it making the transition from closed mouth to open?

Remember that lower notes require you to be very relaxed and open. What might help you to stay relaxed is to visualize yourself as an open channel. You can always refer to chapter 4, The Warrior, to help you or you can create some image for yourself that helps you do this. I like to imagine myself as a tree, rooted in the ground but growing strong and straight toward the sky. The important thing is to clear away tension in the body, so you can breathe and place sound properly. The other component necessary for good voice production is proper physical alignment and posture.

Kristin Linklater, in her insightful book, *Freeing the Natural Voice*, writes:

> You will find that the efficiency of the vocal apparatus depends on the alignment of the body and the economy with which it functions. When the spine is out of alignment its ability to support the body is diminished and muscles intended for other things must provide that support. If the lower spine is weak, the abdominal muscles supply substitute strength for the torso; if the abdominal muscles are employed in holding up the body, they are not free to respond to breathing needs. Similarly, if the upper part of the spine abandons its job of carrying the ribcage and shoulder girdle, the rib muscles may take on the responsibility of holding the chest high, in which case they are unavailable for intercostal breathing. Finally, when the muscles of the neck are not well aligned, the whole channel through which the voice travels is distorted. With a weak neck, the jaw muscles, tongue muscles, laryngeal muscles, even lips and eyebrows become supporters of the head, leaving little chance of a free passage for sound.[3]

[3] *Freeing the Natural Voice* by Kristin Linklater, Drama Books Publishers, New York, N.Y., © 1976, p. 20.

Once again, repeat the placement exercise but this time concentrate on using your face and head resonators.

SOUND-PLACEMENT EXERCISE 4
Discovering Your High Register

1. Relax your mind and body the best you can. Free your arms, shoulders, head and neck.
2. Close your eyes and concentrate on your breathing.
3. Imagine the flow of breath as it passes through you.
4. Feel the natural rise and fall of your abdomen made by the breath.
5. Feel your lungs fill with air.
6. Feel yourself release the air and let it pass through your lips so you can hear it.
7. Now take a breath and release it with sound.
8. Let your lips stay parted and let the sound out on "hee."
9. The sound should be a higher register note, resonating somewhere in or close to the top of your head.
10. Feel the vibration.
11. Focus on where the vibration lives in you. (Try to be precise.)
12. When you have an idea of where the vibration lives, sound the "hee" again. Now repeat the "hee" three times in succession. "Hee, hee, hee." See if you can feel the vibration touch the same place in you each time.
13. Keep your awareness on the vibration.

---

14. Record it in your memory.
15. As you repeated it did it change its location?
16. If it moved, where did it move to?
17. Where would you say this higher "head" sound lives . . . exactly?

In investigating, you might discover certain other aspects of singing that have been or are becoming problematic: namely, your range and your sense of pitch.

Let's examine pitch first. The word pitch actually means, to erect and fix firmly in place; to set a particular level. Pitch refers to the exact height (or depth) of any musical sound according to the number of vibrations that produces it.

As you begin to place your notes upon your internal sound-board, make sure you are relaxed and comfortable. Know that the accuracy of your pitch is dependent largely on two things: how well you hear the pitch and how well you place the note. If you don't hear the note correctly, you obviously have a small chance of reproducing it correctly. If you hear it well but place it badly, you have an equally small chance of reproducing it correctly. Good voice placement is imperative for accurate pitch. So the next time you sing, and are having difficulty with singing on pitch, employ your detective.

Here's an exercise to help you develop your internal sound-board and hone your pitch.

PITCH EXERCISE 1

Using Your Internal Soundboard

1. Stand with your legs apart, one foot slightly in front of the other (this improves balance and guards against shifting hips to adjust to body weight).
2. Close your eyes and focus your attention inward.
3. Hear a musical scale in your head. (If you play an instrument, tape the scale and play it back for yourself during this exercise.)

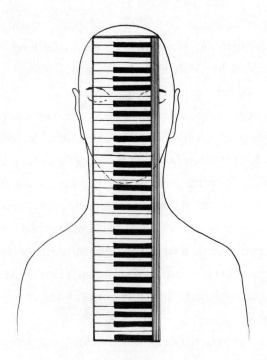

In order to develop and maintain accurate pitch, try imagining a keyboard inside you as you sing. See yourself press the key or pluck the string.

4. Imagine the sounds, as you hear them, inside you. See the vibrations in any manner you like.
5. Now imagine a keyboard. As you hear each pitch, see it being sounded. See yourself press the key or pluck the string. Listen and visualize each tone.
6. On "ah," quietly repeat each tone as you hear it; keeping your focus with your eyes closed, see and feel the tone as you hear it and as you produce it.
7. Now select different tones in the scale randomly. Repeat them as you hear them. Remember to see the tone first and feel the vibration of the tone as you produce it.
8. Relax your focus and take a few comfortable breaths. When you feel ready, open your eyes and bring your attention to the room.

Ask these questions of your detective:

1. Describe your visualization of the keyboard or soundboard that you created.
2. How did this affect your ability in producing sound?
3. How did this affect your sensation of the sound in your body?
4. Are you more or less aware of your resonators?
5. Sing a scale again and notice whether it becomes simpler now that you have created an internal soundboard for yourself.

Remember it is wise at first to simply experiment with different sounds, different pitches, and then allow the natural physical response to occur. Once you feel confident with at least a small spectrum of sound, branch out and test a different part of your voice.

One of my students, we'll call her Elaine, is a great belter. That means she feels most comfortable singing in a low to middle range, which then causes her to "forget" she has an upper register that's quite usable as well. It wasn't until there was a pop song she wanted to sing, which required her to sing higher notes, that she decided to investigate her upper register. At first she was lost and frustrated, because she insisted on approaching that upper register the same way she approached the lower part of her voice, with force and an expectation that the notes would sound in her mouth, throat, and chest. Obviously, this was not working for her. It wasn't until I suggested she gently sigh a couple of high tones that she discovered where those sounds lived. "*Oh!* I feel them now," she said. "They're right here above my eyebrows." "Great," I said. "Now sigh up from there. What do you feel?" She continued to sigh higher tones until she reached the top of her range. She then said, "I feel this pressure at the crown of my head. Wow! I can feel it every time I sing up there." Perfect, I thought. "You did it, Elaine. You broke through to your upper register. Now it's there for the taking."

Sighing is a wonderful tool in finding your voice because it prevents you from pushing. Sighing allows your voice to emerge on its own in its natural form. This becomes invaluable to us when we are trying out new things, such as singing in a higher register.

Let's not forget that pitch and resonance are also influenced by our emotional state. If my student Elaine had had serious reservations about exploring her top register, she might not have been so successful. Emotional conflict causes us to send a mixed message to our brain. The brain in turn becomes unsure how to process an unclear directive. For instance, if you direct your mind to pick up that cup of coffee on the table, your muscles engage, and you reach out and pick up the cup. If, however, you simultaneously direct your brain to not pick up the cup, you experience some difficulty in doing so. You might reach out and then pull back. You might not reach out at all. You might sit and wonder about whether or not you really wanted the cup of coffee. (The next time you procrastinate about doing something, remember this.) Finally, you might reach out, pick up the cup and then spill it before you take a sip. In other words, as we've discussed in chapter 4, The Warrior, you might become engaged in an internal war between both directives—one part of you is fighting for the coffee, the other is fighting against it.

You can see how emotional conflict can complicate the simplest of decisions. Therefore, when you are singing, don't forget to be clear in your intentions. Should you want to expand your range, make sure to explore your feeling about doing so along with actually using exercises to extend your voice. You must believe that you can. The same goes for any aspect of singing. Be clear: Focus in on your desire, then act accordingly.

Here are a few telltale signs of conflicting directives:

1. Excessive tiredness every time you practice
2. Constantly saying, "I can't!" before you attempt to sing
3. Tight jaw and/or inflexible tongue
4. Poor concentration

It's important that you become sensitive to the "clues" as you begin the process of developing your voice. In this way you then know what to do when you reach an impasse and you stop enjoying singing.

PITCH EXERCISE 2

Using Sensory Awareness

1. Stand quietly with your eyes closed and breathe deeply. Place your hands on your waist to make sure you are allowing the breath to cause the natural expansion of your abdomen by pushing the diaphragm down and out. All the while focus on releasing any tension that you might feel. With every breath, be conscious of "breathing out" destructive tension.

2. Now hum a soft tone and let it sound on your lips. Feel the tone dance in and around your mouth. Sustain it only until it's comfortable. Now extend the sound and increase the volume. If this feels uncomfortable, let it go gently, and take another breath. Try to gradually increase the sound in intensity. Make sure it resides primarily in your mouth.

3. Change the shape of the sound to "ah," and then "ee." Then change it back to the original hum.

4. Now change the pitch, raise it by a half step. (If you are not sure about what this sounds like, simply raise the pitch the best you can.)

5. Sing the new pitch on "ah," and then "ee." (If you experience difficulty, always return to the hum.)

---

6. Change the vowel sound to "oh." Let it sound like a sigh of relief. Breathe out any remaining tension.

7. Raise the pitch once more. It should now be approaching the nasal cavity. Concentrate and try to feel it re-sound there.

8. On this pitch, sing "ahhhmmm, ahhhmmm, ahhhmmm." How does closing your mouth affect the resonation of the sound? Does it change its location? Keep a close watch on where it travels to, if it travels.

9. Now, on a long breath let out a sigh from head to toe. Let the breath release slowly.

10. Again, let the breath release slowly and sigh down, joining sound with breath. Keep yourself relaxed.

Continue this exercise by gently raising the pitch each time you start anew. Remember to keep your sensory awareness keen with regard to placement of pitch. Always end with a sigh down, joining sound with breath.

Working the Song

When you feel ready to begin, think about the song you've chosen to sing and read the words aloud. Think about what they're saying. Are they expressing love and desire? Is it a song about losing someone? Is it a joyful, celebratory song or one of sadness and grief? Is it an angry song?

Once you've decided on the message and meaning of the song, say the words aloud once more, reflecting the tone of the text. Next, recite the words once again but extend the sound of the words a little. This is a kind of talk-singing. Keep doing this until you feel a natural transition between speech and song. *Do not think about singing. Think about communicating the ideas in the song.* Try to concentrate solely on the meaning of the text. Keep repeating the words until they feel like your own. Enjoy the rhythm the consonants make. Taste each word. Make the most of every syllable.

Now, sing the song as you know it. *Do not listen to yourself.* Trust that you are singing well. Instead, feel the emotion of the music. Experience the shapes made by the tongue in your mouth. Pay attention to the different vibrations in your face, head, and chest area. Breathe. Breathe. Breathe. Feel the breath's expansions and contractions. Cultivate your energy. Let your energy guide your breath. Let your breath support the sound. Allow yourself to express yourself. Release any fear. Have fun.

After you sing through the song at least once, start to become aware of any vocal problems you might be experiencing. This is your detective's job. When you are sure of what they might be, use the following chart to help you solve them.

Following is a Detective Checklist for when you are having trouble singing and need to solve some basic problems. The clues listed here are samples of what might be happening while you're singing. The questions are supplied so you can begin to figure out why you could be experiencing that particular difficulty. This will point you in the direction to remedy the problem.

Detective Checklist

PROBLEMS WITH BREATHING

CLUE: Your throat is tight and you notice you are straining to reach the note.

    Ask: Do I have enough breath to meet the demands of the phrase?

CLUE: You feel winded, you are having trouble sustaining pitch, you need to take many breaths in just one line of the song.

    Ask: Am I releasing the breath too quickly?

CLUE: The song is fast-paced and you are experiencing difficulty taking breaths in the right place and with enough speed.

    Ask: Do I need to take short catch breaths (breathing high from the chest) or long diaphragmatic breaths?

CLUE: You feel lethargic and your breathing is labored. When you do take a breath, you find you are unable to sustain sound well.

    Ask: Am I employing enough energy?

PROBLEMS WITH MAKING SOUND

CLUE: As you are singing, the tone becomes strident and forced.

    Ask: Am I relaxed enough?

CLUE: You are experiencing pain while singing.

    Ask: Is there tension in my throat? Am I bearing down too hard on my larynx? Is the breath not strong enough to support the sound?

CLUE: You feel as if you are singing with limited range.

    Ask: Do I feel tension anywhere in my body? Where is the tension? How do I release it? Do I have enough energy? Am I forcing the tone? What about the speed of my breath? Am I releasing it quickly enough? Does the sound feel well-placed? (Is it housed in the right place in my body?) How am I visualizing the sound? Am I distracted? How's my concentration?

ARTICULATION AND DICTION

CLUE: You experience slurred speech or diction. You have poor enunciation.

    Ask: Is my tongue flexible? Do I feel any tension in any part of my tongue?

CLUE: You use poor diction. You experience improper voice placement.

    Ask: Am I pronouncing my vowels and consonants correctly? Check your lips and mouth for tension. Review tongue placement for vowel sounds.

CLUE: *Your higher register feels restricted. The "Ee" vowel is difficult to sing. The volume of sound is slight.*

Ask: Is my jaw working efficiently? Does the movement of my jaw feel restricted? Am I dropping my jaw enough for the sound to escape? Does the back of the tongue ride up in my mouth and close the opening in the back of my throat?

I have listed merely a sample of clues and possible leads to solving problems in your singing. Test these and your own by bringing out your chosen song to work on periodically. This will get you in the habit of singing with awareness while not being self-conscious. Know the difference. It's important.

The goal here is to enjoy yourself and to practice singing from the inside out. What do I mean? If you become involved with the emotion inherent in the music and words of the song, you will most likely watch and listen to yourself less. This will make you more free to experience each moment as it comes and you will consequently be more spontaneous and true not only to your delivery of the song, but to yourself.

Your detective is an invaluable partner in life and in song. It will enable you to effectively solve problems and sniff out difficulties as they arise. Self-investigation is not only useful, it is necessary. It yields self-knowledge and self-knowledge builds self-reliance. Self-reliance breeds confidence and in being confident we are free to live and sing as we *like* instead of as we *should.*

THE SPIRITUAL MASTER

CHAPTER SEVEN

THE SPIRITUAL MASTER

"Let your intuition guide you, but let reason speak."

I t was an unusually warm day for late October. The sun shone
brightly. The sky was clear. Renee's face was dewy with excitement. Today was the culmination of years of determination and
hard work. In the past, Renee had only dreamed of a moment
like this one. She had counted the steps, pushed through the finish line in thoughts and daydreams but someday had become now
and now had become real. Today, Renee was going to run the
New York City Marathon. It was just a few hours until her fate as
a runner would be decided.

Renee looked at the sea of faces around her. She wondered
about the other runners. Had they come as far? Were they anything like herself? Renee was thirty-four and a doctor. She was

motivated to run by her own need to heal her damaged knee. Running had once been therapy. Now it was her life.

Getting into starting position, Renee stretched her hamstrings and calf muscles one more time. She closed her eyes, wished softly to herself, "May my natural strength, energy, and ability be available to me today." She simultaneously tightened the ace bandage on her left knee and sighed a gentle sound of relief that this moment was finally here.

The race master shouted a few words and then, with the sound of a gun firing, she started to run. The first five miles were easy. She took them relatively slow. She remembered what Gary, her coach back home in Tucson, used to say, "Save it Renee. Save your strength till the end. You'll need it. Just as you approach the last five miles, you'll be convinced you can't run another. And one more thing," he used to say, "remember to keep your focus. Unite your body, mind, and your spirit. Then you can't lose."

Remembering Tucson and the words of her coach gave Renee a sense of peace. When she brought her attention back to the race, her body was relaxed, her breath was slow and steady and her mind was open.

Then, around the tenth mile, Renee started to become distracted by some voices in her head. "You can't run twenty-five miles. You have a bad knee. You probably won't walk the way you did after your knee operation." It seemed that somehow the race had begun to bring up her past and every doubt she ever felt. Renee remembered her knee as the reason she had wanted to become a doctor in the first place. When she was sixteen, she had been hit by a delivery truck. She had spent six months in the hospital and gone through surgery twice along with rehabilitation. She remembered feeling worthless because her left knee and her right arm were both shattered. She couldn't walk and was dependent on everyone for getting around. During that time, she'd envision herself running the canyon alongside her dog Clara. Those were the only things that kept her sane during those months. But now, as she was here in New York running the race of her life, she wondered why she was thinking about those dark times. She was at her strongest now. Her knee functioned well, if not perfectly. What could be wrong?

Renee forced herself to bring her attention back to the race. The sun was placed high in the sky now and it burned with an orange glare. It was warm. Renee was doing well, but she could feel her breath becoming uneven and her stride followed. It was clear her concentration was waning. Soon, she feared, her energy would be depleted as well.

"I want to win," Renee thought to herself. "I want to win."

"You have already won," a voice inside of her spoke.

"What?" asked Renee, trying to focus on her breath and her stride.

"You have met your match. The test is done," the voice murmured.

Thinking she was dreaming, she opened her eyes wider and picked up her speed. She looked around. Above her she saw the sun burning bright orange, radiating into an aqua sky. "What have I already won?" she wondered.

The sun continued to glisten against the pale sky. Everything around her seemed to sparkle. She could see the smallest parts of glass in the pavement in the road. It appeared Renee had entered into a different state of mind. She no longer felt the road beneath her feet. The sun's glare had turned into a mystical glow. Her head felt light and running was effortless.

In her mind, she returned to seeing herself run and laugh with her dog Clara. Again she heard Clara's bark echo in the canyon. She heard herself saying, "I am strong and joyful." And now as Renee ran, her breath returned to its steady pace and her stride felt long and easy. The miles slipped by. All was going well.

And then it happened. Renee's knee started to ache. At first she ignored it, thinking, "It's only another mile and a half. I can do it." But the pain increased. She started to run putting less pressure on the left leg. Now her whole right side was compensating. Her body was in pain. She looked up at the sun, as if to ask, "What do I do?" It was early afternoon and the light was blinding. The golden sun was ablaze. She started to lose her breath when a strange thing happened. As she was staring into the sun's light, she saw three candles burning. The three flames turned into one and were now one with the sun. She felt her legs stop running. She stood still. The three flames continued to burn into the sun. "Body, mind, and spirit," she said. "That's what it means. I must unite my body, mind, and spirit." She remembered the wisdom of her coach and then a quiet voice inside her asked, "What is your purpose?" While she was thinking, she could feel the other runners passing her by. And still she stood silently. Then the smell of pine and sandalwood filled her senses. The sound of Clara barking in the canyon resounded in her ears. "I am strong and joyful," she said. "I am strong and joyful. My purpose is simply to complete the race."

Renee started to walk toward the finish line. Her limp eased and her walk gradually sped to a slow jog. The finish line was an easy twenty yards away. She smiled and threw her arms up, tilting her head back to the sky.

Renee approached the finish line with her bandaged knee still working and her spirit intact. "I finished." she said. "I ran the marathon and I finished, I won," she murmured again. Just then she remembered her adolescence and her difficulty walking after her knee surgery. She recalled the doctor's words warning her she might not ever resume her normal mobility. And now here she was at the finish line after running twenty-six miles. "I won," she said. "I beat their expectations and I conquered myself."

As we travel along life's path, we can sometimes realize the visions we have created for ourselves and our lives have changed. Renee thought she had a profound desire to win the race. Winning the race would be proof of her strength and healthy, completely healed knee. What she came to realize was that she had already won by deciding early on to run. In deciding to run, she released positive energy, which then moved her to practice and make her muscles strong. By making her muscles strong, her knee would heal gradually and naturally, responding to whatever demands she made of it. By seeing herself healthy, happy, and strong and by stretching and running every day, she was able to accomplish what no one thought possible.

There comes a time in everyone's life, when we must come to grips with our own expectations of ourselves. We must take a serious look at what we want and decide how to achieve it.

What are your expectations of yourself? Are you aware of them? Do these expectations truly belong to you? Or do you feel as though they are someone else's expectations imposed on you?

What is your purpose? Do you know why you work? Why you love? Why you sing? Do you know what you want in your life? Do you know who you are?

Understand one thing: There is a difference between the image you have of yourself and your true self. All of us like to see ourselves in a certain way, thinking we know exactly what it is we want and what it is we're like, but few of us know ourselves that intimately. What does this mean? It usually takes an extraordinary event in our lives to make us realize who we truly are. And when and if we do come to some realization, we sometimes discard or ignore it. Why? It feels much too risky to give up our image of ourselves in favor of some person we've never met . . . our undiscovered self. Those who are regularly involved in some daily practice, be it music, art, running, golf, or yoga, have a better chance at gaining some additional insight and self-knowledge. Why? Because these daily practices, these disciplines require us to require more of ourselves on a day-to-day basis. And in requiring more of ourselves, we are faced with having to accept our limitations while at the same time trying to surpass them.

It is time to welcome your spiritual master.

Your spiritual master is your friend and your teacher. He is your opponent and colleague. He lives inside you, but you must invite him to teach you before he can be heard. His is the voice of wisdom. Not the voice of should's or supposed to's, but the quiet insistent knowing voice that pushes you (if you let it) toward expansion, toward the unknown, past the status quo. Your spiritual master speaks through your hunches, dreams, and fantasies. Your spiritual master is your intuition.

Can you identify your intuition? Do you listen when your intuition speaks? Are you aware of his quiet presence or are you busy distracting yourself with other things? If you are like myself and most of us reading this book, you probably are aware of your intuition occasionally but don't hear him on a daily basis. Or you hear your inner voice often but seldom heed his advice. It's important to realize that we need this voice to be loud and clear and present every day. He is our guide. He will lead the way to a more satisfying, more enjoyable, well-suited life. A good indication of hearing and following this quiet inner presence is that you experience your life with more energy and aliveness. You feel more focused, more peaceful, more forgiving, and less judgmental. But most important, you feel balanced. You feel centered and sure of who to be at each moment. You know when to call on your warrior, scientist, or detective on a moment-to-moment basis. As a spiritual master, you trust your self. You do not require outside validation. And rather than contriving a plan for your life, you allow your life to unfold and you have faith that things will fall into place.

Do you live this way? Of course not! We'd all *like* to live this way but few of us have the nerve. I urge you, however, to take a good look at yourself and figure out how you can start. Why? Because it's time.

Every time you don't follow your inner guidance, you feel a loss of energy, a loss of power, a sense of spiritual deadness.[1]

Because the voice is a channel to the spirit, you will notice that as you continue to grow as a person, your voice will ring with more power and beauty. Singing and speaking will require less effort. Your expression will be the product of intuition and intel-

[1]Shakti Gawain from *The Artist's Way* by Julia Cameron with Mark Bryan, G. P. Putnam's Sons, New York, N.Y., 1992, p. 43.

lect working hand in hand. Your voice is a living barometer of yourself. And because of this, your voice cannot afford the luxury of catering to a self-image. This will only lead you toward its demise—demise of yourself as well as your voice.

Know that the spiritual path is about surrender. Surrender to your intuitive self. Surrender to a more natural way of singing and living. Don't force anything. Effort is required only when we think we ought to do something. It is then that we strive. Striving in life and in singing makes for unhappiness and discomfort. In singing it tenses muscles and shortens breath. It works against our natural inclinations and responses. It separates us from that gentle stirring that infuses us and our voice with energy and individuality, excitement and emotion, beauty and power.

Below is an exercise that I've created to help you connect your breath to your emotions. This is our first step in learning to hear and follow our intuitive voice.

EXERCISE TO CONNECT BREATH TO EMOTIONS

1. Sit quietly in a favorite room of your house or garden.
2. Close your eyes and become aware of your breath.
3. Notice the rise and fall of your abdomen and chest.
4. Allow your mind to wander and watch what is happening there. Do not attempt to control what you see or feel.
5. As different pictures come into view, see them and allow them to pass. Remember to keep the focus on how you feel.

---

6. Stay relaxed as you breathe and then bring your attention to your center. Feel the energy in your body pool in that area.

7. Notice how your center becomes warm when you focus the energy there.

8. Now see the energy disperse into little droplets that move into your arms and hands.

9. Feel your body's reaction.

10. Keep breathing and notice the natural rise and fall of your chest and abdomen.

11. Now disperse the energy throughout your body. See it move and travel through your legs and feet and your torso up to your head and back around.

12. Now check in to see how you're feeling. What are you seeing in your mind?

13. How are you feeling about what you're seeing? Are you able to remain focused and relaxed?

14. Pay attention to what feelings come up and what effect they have on your body and your breathing.

As you do this exercise, try to be aware of any discomfort or pain that you might have. Pain in your body is always a sign of blocked energy. Blocked energy is a sign that something, some issue, has been ignored by you and is definitely "stuck." These "blocks" need to be worked through in order for you to have access to a free and relaxed body and mind. The spirit will have difficulty flowing through you if you do not acknowledge these stymied emotions. Allow your breath to reveal these blocked energies and let it help you release them.

Try the above exercise again, this time focusing the breath on the part of the body which is stiff or in pain. You can also focus it on a part of your body that is simply unresponsive to the breath. Meaning, you can't feel the breath as it passes through that part of your body. When you release the breath through your body, through that part of you which is stiff, unresponsive, or in pain, see and feel the breath massage that part of your body. Ask yourself what it is that is keeping you from freeing that part of yourself. Are you angry? Do you feel sad? Is there a memory attached to the feeling? Begin to allow yourself to see pictures in your mind when you breathe into that hurt area. There is a reason for the discomfort. Let your breath help you connect to it. Your breath can take you straight to the site, straight to the reason, directly to the memory, if you let it. Let it. It will free you and your spirit will be renewed. Not only will you feel better and have more energy but your breath will flow more easily and sound will vibrate and resonate with more ease, clarity and power. And as a result of "breathing through the block," your intuition will visit you more often and you will be more likely to trust it.

As you trust your intuition more and more, a natural balance will begin to take place in your daily life. You will no longer overwork. You will know when you are tired and you will respect that. You will not leave yourself with too little stimulation, you will sense when you need to socialize or to read or to listen to music. You will not panic when problems arise, you will understand who to call upon within yourself to help you find a solution, be it scientist, detective, or warrior. You will realize that each situation that arises in your life will require attention and care and you will call upon your varied personal resources for solutions. You might even feel more able to "go with the flow" if you are not sure about how to proceed. Know that you have everything you need inside yourself in order to function well. And according to Plato, happiness is functioning well. And as a singer, when you are functioning well, your breath is free, your body is strong and healthy and your voice is unencumbered by tension and inhibition. You become a channel for the energy that inhabits you and you express that energy clearly, freely, and without reserve. So the next time you feel a hunch about something, anything, follow it and see what happens. If you don't, you might be very surprised at what might happen.

Just recently, I was out for a stroll with my son. We ran into a friend who invited us up to his house for tea. I declined, despite the fact that I had the sense that we might enjoy tea at that time, because Sam and I were off to the park for our daily late afternoon ritual. When Sam and I got to the park, we proceeded to play and as we were doing so, I slipped and fell with Sam in tow.

"Oh no!" I thought. But before I could do a thing, Sam and I were both flat on the ground.

"Is he hurt?" I asked another parent.

"No. He's fine. How are you?"

"I can't move my arm," I said.

As it turned out, I fractured my elbow and spent the next two days in the emergency room in a nearby hospital. I now am sure that Sam and I were invited for tea for a reason and that my hunch to accept my friend's invitation was a good one. Of course there's never a way of forecasting the future, but even now, I am reminded to take my hunches very seriously—for whatever reason.

As far as music and intuition is concerned, the more we are available to our intuitive selves, the more available we are to our emotions and therefore more able to communicate them through song. Let's remember that music without emotion is an exercise in mechanics and technique, and usually devoid of meaning and beauty.

Take for example some very late twentieth-century music, specifically written as an intellectual exercise. For example, twelve-tone music and minimalism. Its audience is limited to those who are trained to understand this style of composition or those who enjoy the games of the mind. Those who desire to have a more "musical experience" often prefer listening to music of the late-eighteenth and nineteenth centuries (Beethoven, Schumann, Schubert) or pop or jazz, simply because it appeals to the senses and spirit and not just to the mind. As a singer, your power lies in your ability to move yourself and your audience. You must be available to your heart and soul. Think again about those to whom you enjoy listening. It is their heart and spirit you are recognizing and enjoying. Be sure to heed your quiet inner voice.

Your spiritual master is your guide to discovering and using your emotions while at the same time teaching you not to be ruled by them. Trust that if you follow the way of this master, you will stop arbitrarily controlling your body and your voice and consequently will surrender to a more natural self. You will be less dependent on outside validation. And you will be more integrated than ever before. Sound, after all, is a vital part of meditation. In many of the Eastern traditions one chants as one pracitices meditating. Think of personal mantras. Certain sounds are thought to be representative of certain "worlds" in life. For instance, when one sings "hee" high up in the head, this is believed to be the spirit world. When one sings "uh" low, resonating in the chest and stomach, it is representative of the emotional world. "Ah" sung in the middle of the face is attributed to the world of business. It is believed that certain vibrations are representations of different areas of life. As you become more adept at singing with a varied range, you then become more able to discover these different attributes in yourself: physical, mental, and emotional. You live more easily in all worlds, and therefore communicate with a more whole and integrated self. Sound will dissolve blocks and encourage growth and the daily discipline of practicing breathing and singing will help you in discovering and serving your true self. This implies that "the essence of our being is something beyond the physical and mental. It implies that we are all simply creations, or manifestations of that consciousness, which lies beyond the grosser levels of our existence. It is from there that we came, and it is to there that we will return. Through the process of 'evolution' we drop our physical form, and even our mental being, returning to the level of purer consciousness. Out of that consciousness flows manifestation, and manifestation flows back into that consciousness."[2] As a singer it is your responsibility to reflect that consciousness every time you sing. If you can and do, your listeners will be deeply moved and enormously thankful. Because when every note you sing reflects this pure emotion and consciousness, listeners will resonate along with you and be opened up to their own emotions and consciousness as well.

Below is an exercise specifically designed for daily use to expand your consciousness and help you channel your energy into song.

[2]*Science of Breath* by Swami Rama, Rudolph Ballentine, M.D., and Alan Hymes, M.D., The Himalayan Institute of Yoga Science and Philosophy, Honesdale, Pennsylvania, 1979, p. 16.

CHANNELING YOUR ENERGY EXERCISE

1. Every morning (if you are able), provide yourself with some quiet time.
2. Sit upright with your back straight and your arms resting at your sides.
3. Close your eyes and allow yourself to breathe naturally.
4. Watch your breath and notice your emotional state.
5. If you are nervous or upset or angry, don't try to change your emotion.
6. Continue to breathe and watch your breath until the physical manifestation of the emotion begins to lessen.
7. At this point, sing the first line of the song you've chosen to work on.
8. Feel your emotion gather in the center of your body.
9. Now allow what you are feeling to permeate the music and color the words by having the breath transport the emotion along with your sound.

You must visualize this. Some examples are given on the following pages.

10. Sing from from the center of your body, seeing the emotion fuse with your breath. Feel the sensations in your body created by breath, emotion, and sound. Make note of what you are feeling.
11. Continue to sing the song, with your focus on your breath and feeling the sound inhabit your body.

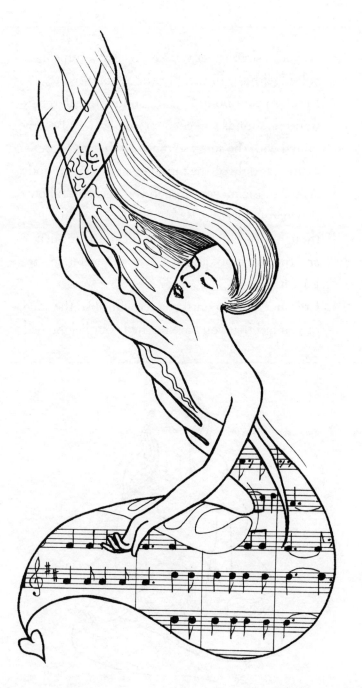

Channel your energy into song. Allow what you are feeling to permeate the music and color the words.

12. As you're singing, let your awareness become involved with the music. Breathe as you need to. Listen to your body. Feel the sound. Let all the extraneous sounds you encounter fade away. Become united with the song, so much so that you have awareness only of the music inhabiting your body.

13. As the music moves through you, feel and follow the energy traveling. Remember to allow any thought or feeling other than the music to surface and then let it go quickly. See it and feel it and release it.

14. Continue singing until you have finished the song or you feel that you have reached your heightened

Allow energy to come through you.

state for the time being. (Ideally, your heightened state will include a surge of energy. Your body and voice will warm. You might break a sweat, or you may just feel peaceful.)

Repeat this exercise as often as you like, preferably in the morning before you start your day, or in the evening before you retire.

Keep in mind that being a spiritual master implies weeks, months, or even years of daily practice. After some time, the discipline at hand, whether it is singing, yoga, or meditation, becomes wholly integrated in your being. It becomes a part of you and you will no longer need to practice it in the same way. In your pursuit, you will find the keys to who you are and how you are to be in the world.

You would be wise to honor discipline. It will teach you, humble you, and comfort you. Discipline in the form of daily practice will ultimately free you. Every artist and athlete knows that no matter how much raw talent is available to them, without daily pracitice, the art or game is never quite as accomplished as it could be. They also understand that within the practice of the form is found the self. Living is about process. Learn to enjoy it and you will forever be content. Ignore it and you are doomed to continually hunt for the pot of gold at the end of the rainbow. And as we well know, gold is rarely worth what we think it is once we have it. Savor the moment.

THE SINGER

CHAPTER EIGHT

THE SINGER

"My heart is a song that I need to sing."

Albert sat upon the rocks looking out at the sea curl its foamy legs around the shore. Each wave brought the sound of water, movement, and seagulls clamoring for clams. The sky was silver gray with the hint of yellow peeking out behind cottony clouds. "All is well with the world," he thought. "All is well." At that instant another sound joined in with the crashing waves and seagulls. It was a warm sound, fluid and bright. It took Albert by surprise and he smiled when he heard it. It reminded him of home, where he would sit for hours by the beach and listen to the Spanish music of his family. Nothing could make him feel happier than hearing these songs while dreaming by the ocean.

Albert was singing. And by this time he was singing in full voice. "I'm singing an ode to the sea," he thought. And then he laughed. "How absurd I should be singing to no one." But it didn't stop him. He kept on, remembering the family tradition.

His father had been a singer and saxophone player back in Puerto Rico, where Albert was born. His mother was a classical guitarist and all three of his sisters were singers and pianists. Albert, however, insisted that music was not to be his livelihood and so entered law school in America. Now he was a successful attorney living in San Diego. But as Albert sat there on the beach far from his office and phone, his spirit seemed to surface in a song.

"I must be crazy," he said to himself. He looked at his watch and realized lunch was becoming the better part of the afternoon. But returning to the office didn't seem feasible now. He was having too much fun.

Albert started to experiment with all different sorts of sounds. The vibrations his voice was making were almost as pleasing to him as feeling the ocean's salty spray wash against his face. He sang long legato lines with little breath in between followed by short staccato phrases where his tongue touched the roof of his mouth in quick, pointed movements. He sang in English and in Spanish and allowed himself to dance to the music he was making. He felt his heart beat in rhythm with the pulse of the song. He heard himself soar above the sounds of the sea and cried with ecstasy. As he sang, he felt his voice take flight like the birds flying above him. Singing way up high, he blessed the earth for inspiring him as it did. Then he lowered his voice, feeling his trunk vibrate like an electric motor. His body felt good. His mind was relaxed. His spirit ignited. Albert was blissfully engaged in song.

"Why don't I do this more often?" he asked himself. "It feels great!" He then remembered a young woman by the name of Annuela, to whom he had taken a fancy when he was in college. Each night they'd sing songs and play music long into the morning. It was comforting in its similarity to the nights he'd spent singing with his own family. In both cases, some days were spent sleeping just to recover from all the frolicking the night before. Annuela was going to be a singer, she used to tell him. "I wish you well," said Albert. "I cannot say I will do the same."

When Annuela and Albert parted their senior year, he buried himself in books and the law. There was little time for anything else. Secretly, he admitted missing the music of his family and Annuela but he never spoke of either.

Albert was silent now. He turned away from the ocean and began retracing his steps toward the parking lot. It was late and Albert decided not to return to the office. This was unlike him, but something had changed that day.

The drive home was peaceful. The sky became dark and the stars shone like precious jewels set on black velvet. Albert began to sing again. This time the sound flooded his senses. He felt his throat open wide and through this unobstructed instrument came colors and range he had never before experienced. His head felt light from deep breathing and his face tingled with vibration.

"I shall never stop," he said sighing. "No matter where or how, I shall always sing. *Mi corazón es una canción que necesito cantar.* (My heart is a song that I need to sing. I shall always sing.)" he promised.

Albert arrived home and called his family in old San Juan. He told his father he would be visiting at Christmas. He said he would be joining them at the city's festival where his family has sung for decades. *"Bueno, mi hijo. Hasta luego, vaya con Dios y escucha, por favor, a su música.* (Very well, my son. Until then, go with God and listen, please, to His music.)"

Albert hung up the phone, took out his guitar, and sang. "All is right with the world," he said. "All is right with the world."

Discovering Your Joy

Albert was overtaken by the sheer beauty of the landscape. He could not contain his joy, which fed his spirit and which caused him to sing. Beyond his own wishes, he felt compelled to emote in sound. Albert had to acknowledge his heart and soul and he did so in song. There was no choice. There was no other way.

What is it that stirs you? What gets you excited to be alive? A melody can speak a thousand words. Harmony can be translated into many languages. A song, as we have seen, can express the inexpressible.

But most important and beyond anything else that has previously been discussed, you must first consider what moves you before you can sing. Live your joy first. Then sing it. It will come naturally to you once you feel energized by living a satisfying life. Your voice will flow freely out of a life shaped and molded by your own values, taste, and choices. It does not matter whether you feel happy or sad, angry or not—it matters simply that you feel.

It is your personal responsibility to yourself to discover what inspires you. You can only hope to move someone else if you yourself are moved. If you don't really know what moves you or if you are unsure, you can discover this in several ways. You will know that you are moved by the distinct physical changes in your body. You will most definitely experience a sense of aliveness and increased energy. You will feel happy, almost giddy, like a child eating his first ice-cream cone. You might even feel lightheaded from joy. Keep in mind, though, that it might take a while before you allow yourself to get to that point. And you may encounter some fear and anger along the way. Following is an exercise designed to help you get to know what moves you.

EXERCISE FOR DISCOVERING YOUR JOY

1. My favorite way to spend the day is _____ .
2. I often dream of traveling to _____ .
3. If given a chance to read a mystery, novel, or biography, I would choose _____ .
4. The music I enjoy listening to is _____ .
5. I love to sing _____ in my _____ .
6. If given the chance, I'd build my house in _____ .
7. I often dream of having _____ .
8. I wish I could feel good about _____ .
9. I cry when I feel _____ .
10. I laugh when _____ .
11. I need to communicate because _____ .
12. I want to sing because _____ .

After you fill in the blanks, sit and meditate awhile on how you've completed these statements. Were you honest? Is there something else you'd like to add? Do you have any negative feelings about discovering your joy? If you do, make note of them in the journal that you've been using throughout this book. Be sure to recognize any and all feelings as they will aid you in uncovering your spirit and your heart. And as I've mentioned before, it is precisely your spirit and your heart that are required for powerful singing. If you fail to recognize these feelings, you are sure to create resistance and blocks for yourself, which will only impede your growth later on. These blocks often manifest themselves by creating closed throats and hard-to-manage breathing styles. As a singer you cannot afford these blocks, which most assuredly will stop you from singing. Try to be thorough and honest with yourself. Your voice is depending on you.

Knowing the Form

In addition to understanding what moves you, you must also understand *what* you are singing. Do you understand what the lyricist had in mind when he/she wrote that particular song? Are you aware of the musical meaning supporting the lyrics?

You don't have to be a musician or a poet to appreciate the rise and fall of a musical line. Or the witty rhyme of the last line of the chorus of a song. Or the uncanny match between music and text. You can most certainly sing by not realizing any of these things; however, learn a little about song form, lyrics, and phrasing and you'll be able to sing with more confidence and flair. And best of all, you'll feel more comfortable about making choices on how to deliver a song.

Working the Song

Take out the song you've chosen to work on and place the music on a desk or table. (If you are working from memory, write the words down on a white, ruled piece of paper.) Make sure you have a pencil and a pad (your journal perhaps) as well. If you'd like to listen to the song you've chosen to work on, tape yourself singing it and use that as a guide. (You may listen to other artists sing it, but we are trying to avoid comparisons. Trust yourself to make the correct decision.)

On your piece of paper draw a box and divide it into four columns so it looks like the one that follows.

Label the sections as follows: Lyric, General Meaning, Personal Significance, and Music's Direction. This is going to be your worksheet for discovering the meaning and power of this particular song.

Here's how it works:

1. Write out the line or lines of the song you wish to work on in the appropriate column.

Lyric	General Meaning	Personal Significance	Music's Direction

2. Then interpret its general meaning and write it in its appropriate column. (Translate the line as if you were speaking to a child or person speaking a foreign language.)

3. Now think about what the line means to you personally. Write it down.

4. Under Music's Direction, plot out, like points on a graph, how the music moves up or down or whether it stays constant.

5. Then notate its location on a representation of your body.

The following chart is given as an example.

Lyric	General Meaning	Personal Significance	Music's Direction
Are you going to Scarborough Fair? Parsley, Sage, Rosemary and Thyme. Remember me to one who lives there. He once was a true love of mine.	If you are going to the fair, will you please let this person know I am thinking about them and that he/she has always been fondly remembered.	This reminds me of Steven. I feel so sorry that we broke up. I wonder how he is and whether he still loves me. I long to see him.	

The purpose of this exercise is to help you decipher a song so that not only are you familiar with the words and music, but you have thought about each line and "practiced" saying the words to yourself and "placing" each tone in your body as well.

Let's not forget that our technical facility is an important component in learning to master a particular piece of music. Those of us who have coaches and teachers may rehearse a song for months with an accompanist before we dare sing it aloud to anyone else. But it is not necessary, nor is it wise for this to be your only method of learning to perform. And especially for those who have no other means to "practice," this exercise is helpful and sometimes alarmingly informative.

By defining how a lyric is personally significant to you, you will uncover hidden feelings and fantasies about a whole host of things. As you do this you will begin to feel freer and/or you may experience fear about proceeding. In any case, these revelations are valuable to you in the sense that they will guide you toward what your next step in your musical journey needs to be. For instance, if you realize that while singing "Are You Going to Scarborough Fair?" you start thinking about your best friend in high school, or you imagine moving to California, or you feel peaceful and serene, you have discovered something real and important about your feelings and desires connected to that song. How? You have found a bridge to your unconscious. Allow yourself to remain open and the associations will come. Their meaning— how you interpret them—is up to you. What the feelings will do for you, however, is help you ignite the song with urgency and a sense of purpose. These associations will lend the song a certain specificity that it could not have without your particular feelings about it.

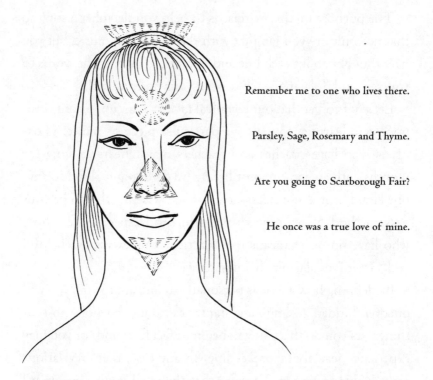

Remember me to one who lives there.

Parsley, Sage, Rosemary and Thyme.

Are you going to Scarborough Fair?

He once was a true love of mine.

Notate the location of each musical line on a representation of your face and body.

Make the Music Yours

In Constantin Stanislavski's book, *An Actor Prepares,* he quotes a teacher of his saying, "It is true that the great poets and artists draw from nature. But they do not photograph her. Their product passes through their own personalities and what she gives them is supplemented by living material taken from their store of emotion memories."[1]

[1] *An Actor Prepares* by Constantin Stanislavski, pub. by Theatre Arts Books, New York, N.Y. © 1936, p. 163.

"Music is," Charlie Parker once said, "your own experience, your thoughts, your wisdom. If you don't live it, it won't come out your horn."[1] Remember—singing is all about you and how you choose to communicate a particular piece of music wedded to a particular lyric. Also remember that what a song is *about* is conveyed to an audience by the choices you make as the singer.

Phrasing

One of those all important choices you must make as a singer is how you decide to phrase a song.

A phrase is a sequence of words conveying a thought. A musical phrase could be considered a sequence of notes conveying a thought or a small group of notes forming a definite melodic or thematic feature in a composition. In any case, as the singer, you must first acknowledge the thought and then choose how to communicate it. This choice can be made in several ways: You can follow the sense of the lyric at hand, and take a breath each time a new thought begins, or you may follow the music and breathe after a resolution to a climax or when the musical thought feels complete. Phrasing is the art of articulating and shaping the various elements of the musical parts (words and music). Good phrasing includes the observance of tied (held) or detached groupings of notes, the distribution of stresses and inflections, breath control and diction. Very often what makes singing most interesting is the manner in which a singer phrases a given

[1]Charlie Parker from *The Artist's Way* by Julia Cameron with Mark Bryan, G. B. Putnam's Sons, New York, N.Y., 1992, p. 159.

melody. In learning to phrase a melody, it is important to first understand the concept of melody and its components.

Melody and Phrasing

When we talk of melody in song, it usually refers to the musical line that we sing. We use the term musical line because upon examining the melody of a piece or song, one notices a distinct beginning, middle, and end comprised of many notes. In fact this line, consisting of a series of tones, higher and lower, faster and slower, are strategically placed so they work together toward a goal—a climax—and then eventually toward a resolution or conclusion. A melody is similar to the plot of a dramatic piece. It is the theme of a musical work. The melody also carries words which, in addition to the music, help us convey thoughts and feelings. Melody translates the meaning of a song to an audience. Some of the musical techniques that composers use in creating climaxes and resolutions are repetition, range, and musical tension created by ascending sections and dissonant harmonies, followed by descending passages and consonant cadences that create relaxation and resolution. A melodic line may be described as angular or smooth, tense or relaxed, energetic or languid. Above all, a melody must be interesting. We say of a painter that he has a sense of line, meaning that he is able to sustain movement over the whole of his canvas. The same holds true for the unfolding rising and falling melody line.

As singers, our responsibility to the music is to provide the most appropriate performance of this existing musical line. We must notice and understand the "peaks" and "valleys" and be able to travel the distance without unnecessary interruption. This means our breathing, and our articulation of a given line will be determined by not only the text of the song but by the melodic structure as well.

Take out the chart that you made for your practice song and look at the motion of the melody. This time I'd like you, on a separate page, to chart the motion again, but this time do it along with the words to the song.

The following is an example of this technique:

Are you going to Scarborough Fair?

Parsley, sage, rosemary and thyme.

Remember me to one who lives there.

He once was a true love of mine.

When you have completed charting the motion of the melody along with its accompanying lyrics, start to decide where you might take your breaths to shape the phrases. You will want to make these phrases easy to understand and not too challenging for yourself in terms of breathing. Give yourself a break and start slow. For practical purposes, you can mark your breaths with a mark such as ^ or underline the phrase and then discontinue the line at the point at which you breathe.

See the following example:

Are you going to Scarborough Fair?^
Parsley, sage, rosemary and thyme.^

or:

Remember me to one who lives there.
He once was a true love of mine.

Learning to phrase correctly is a lifelong job. It is a talent worth cultivating though, because as we've previously discussed, good phrasing is often the earmark of a seasoned and talented singer. Listening to singers famous for their phrasing is also a good idea. A few of them are: Frank Sinatra, Ella Fitzgerald, and k.d. lang. Listen to some of their music. Take notes and try some of their tricks. Don't copy them, simply observe, listen and practice. Allow the masters, if you can, to inspire you without intimidating you. We all need heroes. But don't forget to trust yourself above everyone else. Be true to your instrument.

A Note about Song Form and Rhythm

Many popular songs as well as theatre songs are written to conform to a specific structure. For instance there exists a form that's popularly referred to as AABA. This particular form is organized in such a way that the first part of the song is repeated (A,A) and it is then followed by a contrasting section (B), returning to a section similar to or exactly the same as the first section (A). Hence, AABA. A good example of AABA form is "Someone to Watch Over Me" by George and Ira Gershwin.

Below is the lyric with its highlighted sections.

A There's a somebody I'm longing to see.
    I hope that he turns out to be,
    Someone who'll watch over me.

A I'm a little lamb who's lost in the wood.
    I know I could always be good.
    To someone who'll watch over me.

B Although he may not be the man some girls think of as
        handsome.
    To my heart he carries the key.

A Won't you tell him please to put on some speed,
    follow my lead, oh how I need,
    Someone to watch over me.

Comprehending song form is helpful to the singer in a myriad of ways. The two most important reasons are as follows:

I. It's always important to have an understanding of the form in which you are working. A writer of short stories should be familiar with those authors who are famous for these types of stories, such as writings by O. Henry and Isaac Bashevis Singer. The "architecture" of this type of writing is vastly different from that of lengthy novels and more different still from poetry.

2. Understanding song form will inform your choices concerning phrasing, flourishes, dynamics, tempo, and dramatic intention as well. If you are singing a song whose form is AAAA, like that of a lot of folk music, you will most definitely be faced with the dilemma of how to make the song interesting and exciting to the listener. And since it will be challenging, due to the fact that there is a lot of repetition, you will have to be not only knowledgeable, but clever in your delivery. A great singer is one who can "fool" an audience into thinking they are listening to a more involved piece of music than actually exists.

Other examples of different song forms are: ABAB, AAA, AABACA, and Verse, Chorus, Verse, Chorus. The latter is most often used in popular songs. Following is a sample Verse Chorus song.

Yankee Doodle
by Dr. Richard Shuckburgh

VERSE   Yankee Doodle went to town
A-riding on a pony.
Stuck a feather in his hat
And called it macaroni.

CHORUS   Yankee Doodle keep it up,
Yankee doodle dandy,
Mind the music and the step,
And with the girls be handy.

VERSE   Father and I went down to camp,
Along with Captain Gooding,

There we saw the men and boys,
As thick as hasty pudding
CHORUS   Yankee Doodle keep it up,
Yankee doodle dandy,
Mind the music and the step,
And with the girls be handy.

etc.

Take a look at your journal now and outline the form of the song you are working on. Think about what choices you need to make in order to better represent the words and music. Do you need to vary the phrasing and dynamics a bit to make it more interesting? Or is the song rather complex and would you do better to simplify your presentation so as to welcome the listener? Decide what it is you must do and make the necessary notations in your book or on the music. Deciphering the shape of the song will give you a path to follow. It's like having your personal road map, complete with instructions to your destination. And by having a path to follow, you will most likely reach your destination successfully. Where is your destination? You have reached your destination once you have achieved an effective representation of words and music. What is an effective representation of words and music? An effective representation of words and music begins with an actively involved performer, willing to be open, ready to be moved. It continues with a telling of a story or conveyance of a message resulting in an engaged audience changed by the experience. You will have to sharpen your skills and talents so that you can serve the song. That's the key. Serve the song the best way you know, and you will be surprised by the dramatic results. How does one best serve the song?

There's an old joke about someone asking how to get to Carnegie Hall. The man who was asked replies, "Practice! Practice!"

Practicing

The most effective and enjoyable way to practice is to devise a method that's right for you. Ask yourself:

1. Which time of day am I most relaxed, refreshed, and awake?
2. Where do I like to be when I sing? In the shower, by the piano, outside?
3. What are my feelings about being true to the process every day by being consistent?
4. Am I able to be consistent?
5. What exercises yield the most positive results for me?

Acknowledge that everyone's process is different and each of us requires respect with regard to our differences.

On the following pages are groups of exercises designed to strengthen your instrument and to help you gain a sense of competence and completion. If the exercises seem too difficult or confusing for you, simply refer back to prior chapters and redo the exercises highlighted in the book. Then return to this chapter and try again. It might also be helpful, if you don't read music or play an instrument, to garner support from a friend or family member who does. Tape the music part of the exercise and practice every other day with the tape. Make sure you don't use the tape every day, because you don't want to get too dependent on the musical accompaniment.

Proceed with courage, curiosity, and self-determination. But keep in mind that learning is distressing as much as it is enjoyable, tedious as well as engrossing, frightening as well as exciting. And remember that progress is never steady. But as long as you have a heart that needs to sing, you have nothing to lose but the excuses why you can't. My final word is *"Sing!"*

Vocal Exercises

BREATH EXERCISES

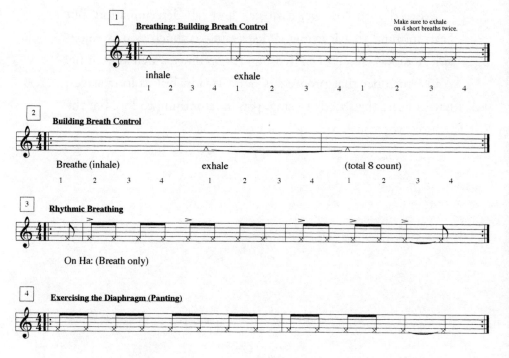

1 **Breathing: Building Breath Control**

Make sure to exhale on 4 short breaths twice.

inhale   exhale
1 2 3 4   1 2 3 4   1 2 3 4

2 **Building Breath Control**

Breathe (inhale)   exhale   (total 8 count)
1 2 3 4   1 2 3 4   1 2 3 4

3 **Rhythmic Breathing**

On Ha: (Breath only)

4 **Exercising the Diaphragm (Panting)**

Note: On all the above exercises, sound may be added after breathing exercises have been completed.

SOUND EXERCISES

General Note: These exercises are written in a female register. Men should start singing one octave lower.

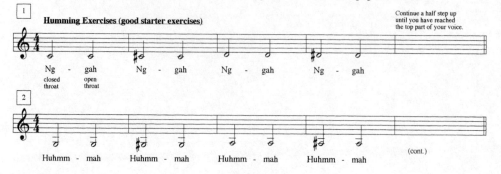

1 **Humming Exercises (good starter exercises)**

Continue a half step up until you have reached the top part of your voice.

Ng - gah   Ng - gah   Ng - gah   Ng - gah
closed open
throat throat

2

Huhmm - mah   Huhmm - mah   Huhmm - mah   Huhmm - mah   (cont.)

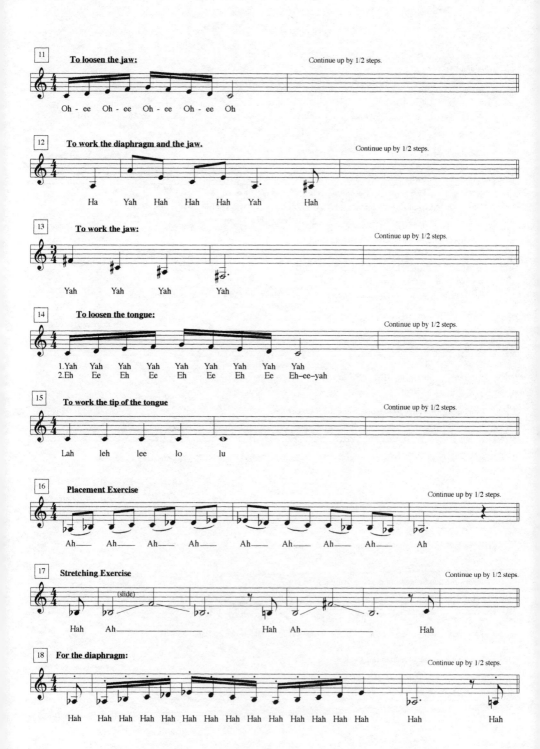

EPILOGUE

In looking for some additional words to give you, I thought long and hard about what other information I could impart to you that might be useful. Sure, I could supply you with additional exercises, I could stress the importance of consistent study, I could talk about my experience as a singer. But all of that seemed unimportant compared to sharing with you the variable nature of life and music.

As you go through each day, you will find each experience you have is seen and felt with a somewhat different pair of eyes and a slightly changed heart. As you grow, you cannot feel as you have felt before simply because you are created and re-created by your choices, circumstances, and your cumulative experiences every day you live. A song is very much like a day. It cannot be experienced the same way twice. And because each day, each song remains ever changing despite its similarity in structure and form, neither I nor anyone else can give you a definitive set of rules or suggestions by which to live or by which to sing. Perhaps the most valuable thing to note is: The ever-changing nature of music, along with the ever-changing nature of a life cannot be captured or contained simply and absolutely. Yes, a song is written. The notes are fixed upon the page, the meter established and the lyric stated. Yes—a life is lived by a person with a name, a profession, an address, a race, a color, religion, and culture. But beyond the external markings of music and the outermost trappings of a life lies an abstract form, and quiet heart waiting to be expressed. Both expect to be expressed with love, with compassion, grief or anger, joy or tears. The song sits longingly, the heart beats quietly. Both anticipate their true birth—one where breath meets sound, one where sound meets emotion, and where emotion finally gives way to music.

It is my sincere hope that during the course of this book, I have succeeded in showing you that music can help you awaken your curiosity, increase your powers of observation and encourage you to experiment along with deepening your sense of feeling and awareness. If this has happened, even in the smallest of increments, then I feel satisfied knowing you have welcomed the process and will undoubtedly and ultimately be transformed by it.

Trust that you know. Be confident in what and how you feel. Remember life is a song that cannot be fixed upon a page. It must be sung and can only be sung by you. In the words of songwriter Joe Raposo:

Sing.
Sing a song.
Make it simple,
to last your whole life long . . .
Don't worry that it's not good enough,
for anyone else to hear.
Just sing.
Sing a song.